Die Reihe „Weltwirtschaft und internationale Zusammenarbeit" wird herausgegeben von

Prof. Dr. Hartmut Sangmeister, Hochschule für Wirtschaft, Technik und Kultur (HWTK), Berlin
Prof. (em.) Dr. Oskar Gans, Universität Heidelberg
Prof. Dr. Detlef Nolte, GIGA Institut für Lateinamerika-Studien Hamburg

Band 14

Junhong Meng

Chinese Rural Banking Situation and the Reform of the Main Rural Financial Supplier
Rural Credit Cooperatives

 Nomos

Promoted by means of the Deutscher Akademischer Austauchdienst (DAAD).

Dle Deutsche Nationalbibliothek lists this publication in the
Deutsche Nationalbibliografie; detailed bibliographic data
is available in the Internet at http://dnb.d-nb.de

a.t.: Heidelberg, Univ., Diss., 2014

ISBN: HB   978-3-8487-1499-5
         ePDF   978-3-8452-5541-5

British Library Cataloguing-in-Publication Data
A catalogue record for this book is available from the British Library.

ISBN: HB   978-3-8487-1499-5

Library of Congress Cataloging-in-Publication Data
Meng, Junhong
Chinese Rural Banking Situation and the Re-form of the Main Rural
Financial Supplier *Rural Credit Cooperatives*
Junhong Meng
192 p.
Includes bibliographic references and index.

ISBN   978-3-8487-1499-5

1. Edition 2014
© Nomos Verlagsgesellschaft, Baden-Baden, Germany 2014. Printed and bound in
Germany.

Editor's preface

In spite of the rapid urbanisation process, which has taken place in the People's Republic of China in recent years, the majority of the population is still living in rural areas. However, rural areas as well as the population working and living there have been disregarded by the Chinese policy aiming at catch-up industrialisation for a long time. As a result, there is a complex set of problems often described as the "Three Rural Issues" in the political debate; what is meant are the interdependent problems of rural areas, agriculture and the farming population. This set of problems has created an exceedingly complex situation in China's rural areas and contributed to the increasing dissatisfaction among the rural population.

Against this background, the Communist Party of China (CPC) and the State Council of the People's Republic of China have first proclaimed, in 2002, the creation of a "modestly prosperous society", and in 2006 the building of a "harmonious society". Whether it will be possible to meet those objectives depends, among others, on whether and how the "Three Rural Issues" will be solved. The Chinese Central Government has drafted a set of measures in order to modernise Chinese agriculture and simultaneously improve the living conditions of the rural population in a sustainable manner. Those measures comprise all fields of agricultural policy and its implementation on different levels of the public administration system, the state pricing policy, public investment in agriculture and rural areas, public services in rural areas, as well as the agricultural financing system.

An in-depth analysis of the last-mentioned part of the modernisation strategy is the core of this study, presented by *Junhong Meng* as her PhD-Thesis at the University of Heidelberg/Germany. By means of this analysis, the author wants to offer a description of the status quo of the rural financial institutions in China and analyse the effectiveness of the institutional reforms of financial service providers in rural areas conducted so far.

The most important financing institutions in China's rural areas and their considerable importance for the agriculture are described extensively: the major state-owned banks in the agricultural sector, the small rural credit cooperatives (RCCs), as well as new types of rural financial service providers. Moreover, readers will discover how national banking supervision in China is organised institutionally and towards which major criteria for credit transactions it is geared: the level of capitalisation of banks, liquidity risks, credit risks and profitability risks.

In her study, the author has put special emphasis on the reforms of RCCs, traditionally playing a decisive role in the financing of the agriculture and rural population in China. However, the tasks and functions of RCCs have changed considerably in the course of the market-oriented commercialisation and privatisation of financial service providers in China's rural areas. This is evidenced by the detailed description of the history of RCCs and their changeful economic performance during the last 20 years. Actually, those credit cooperatives have at best been in accordance with cooperative principles in their early years. Since 1996, the Chinese Central Government has tried to address the menace of declining credit cooperatives due to unclear ownership rights and liability, widespread mismanagement and clientelism by means of a set of reforms. The main objectives of this first set of reforms were the separation between the RCCs and the state-owned Agricultural Bank of China, which had been absorbing the RCCs' losses so far; as well as providing for a higher level of responsibility of local RCC shareholders for the economic success of their credit transactions.

Since 2003, further steps in the RCC reform process have been taken as the previous measures had only partly fulfilled the expectations of a better economic performance of RCCs. Those reform measures included among others the decentralisation of decision-making and a greater involvement of local political players and CPC's officers into the management of rural credit cooperatives. Initially, those reforms steps have only been tested and are being tested in particular pilot provinces. Regrettably, little emphasis was put on the identification of possible weaknesses in the conception of those processes and even less emphasis on visible losses of efficiency in the implementation of those reforms on the operational level of rural financing systems.

According to the author, the question still remains whether the now commercially oriented RCCs are better suited for fulfilling the financial requirements in China's rural areas and whether the poor population also has access to those profit-oriented financial service providers still playing a major role in the field of financing services on rural financial markets in China. Conceptual weaknesses of the reform processes as well as thlosses of efficiency in the implementation of those reforms on the operational

6

level of rural financing systems are evident.

What has been largely left out of account are the political economy of reform processes introduced by the central government, how those reforms are also applied for securing the CPC's monopoly on power as well as the integration of the reforms in the general societal context in China and the difficult process of transformation it is undergoing. However, if this study is seen as a mere analysis of banking reform management, it provides substantial insights concerning the difficulty and complexity of modernisation processes in rural financing systems in emerging countries such as China.

To put her study on a firm empiric footing, Junhong Meng has assembled and analysed relevant banking statistics and investigated an impressive amount of laws, decrees, documents and statements released by the relevant CPC's organs and competent state institutions in China. The author's analysis contributes without any doubt to a better understanding of the complex reform process of rural financing institutions in China.

Heidelberg, March 2014   Hartmut Sangmeister

Acknowledgements

This book is the final work of my PhD studies at the Faculty of Economics and Sozial Sciences of Ruprecht-Karls University Heidelberg from Februry 2010 to February 2014. The four-year research experience is for me life-long unforgettable and I have earned a lot during this process. I love the city Heidelberg and the people I met there. Here I want to take the chance to thank following people, who are for me very important.

The first person I want to grant my thanks is Prof. Dr. Hartmut Sangmeister from Heidelberg University. He is my supervisor during my PhD studies. I own him a lot of thanks. First I want to thank him for taking me as his doctor student so that I can have the opportunity to begin with my research in Germany. Furthermore, I want to thank him for integrating me to the "working group of development policy" and offering me a lot of possibilities to know more about this research direction. I also thank him sincerely for his valuable and constructive commands and suggestions to my dissertation. Thank him so much for all his steady help and support in the last four years. It's a fortune for me to have him as my supervisor.

I'm also indebted to Prof. Dr. Switgard Feuerstein, who is the second supervisor of my thesis. I thank her for taking time to read my thesis and thank her a lot for all her help and support in last four years.

I want to thank all the colleges in the "working group of development policy" of Heidelberg University. They are Julia Rückert, Erika Günther, Alexa Schönstedt, Katja Hilser and Bernd Lämmlin. This is an inspiring and enjoyable group. I really appreciate their support during my whole stay in Germany and it is a very worthy experience to learn from each of them.

My sincere thanks also go to the DAAD, which has supported my stay in Germany financially. At last, I want to thank my dear mother, father and my lovely grandmother for all their support and love in my whole life. I want to thank my friends Xi Chen, Ruoming Wu, Qiang Zhu, Maren Sobottka and many other friends, who have ever helped me.

Heidelberg, April 2014   Junhong Meng

Content

Abbreviations

A-IRB	Advanced internal rating-based (approach)
ABC	Agricultural Bank of China Limited
ADB	Asian Development Bank
ADBC	Agricultural Development Bank of China
AMC	Asset management company
Basel I	Basel Capital Accord of 1988
Basel II	New Basel Capital Accord of 2004
Basel III	Basel Capital Accord (2010-2011)
BIS	Bank for International Settlements
BOC	Bank of China
BOCOM	Bank of Communications
CAR	Capital adequacy ratio
CBRC	China Banking Regulatory Commission
CCB	China Construction Bank
CCBs	City commercial banks
CIRC	China Insurance Regulatory Commission
CSRC	China Securities Regulatory Commission
ECB	European Central Bank
FIs	Financial institutions
FSB	Financial Stability Board
ICBC	Industrial and Commercial Bank of China Limited
IPO	Initial public offering
JSCB	Joint-stock commercial bank
n.a.	not available
NDRC	National Development and Reform Commission
NGOs	Non-Governmental Organizations
NPC	National People's Congress
NPLs	Non-performing loans
PBC	People's Bank of China
PRC	People's Republic of China
PSBC	Postal Savings Bank of China
PSRB	Postal Savings and Remittance Bureau
RCBs	Rural commercial banks
RCCs	Rural credit cooperatives
RCFs	Rural co-operative foundations
RcoBs	Rural cooperative banks

Abbreviations

RFIs	Rural financial institutions
RMB	Renminbi (Chinese currency, also CNY or Yuan)
ROA	Return on assets
ROE	Return on equity
SAFE	State Administration of Foreign Exchange
Sannong	Agriculture, rural areas and peasants
SIFI	System important financial institution
SME	Small and medium enterprise
SOCB	State-owned commercial bank
SOEs	State-owned enterprises
TVEs	Township and village enterprises
UCCs	Urban credit cooperatives
VTBs	Village and township banks

List of tables

List of figures

List of boxes

1. Introduction

Since the implementation of reform and opening up policy in 1978, China has successfully transformed from a centrally planned economy to a market economy. The other transition that occurred at the same time is a structural transformation from an agriculture-based to a non-agriculture-based economy. During the early stage of the transformation, China has continued its mono-bank system until 1983 so that the funds necessary for industrialization could be centrally allocated to support the special sectors. This concentrated use of funds contributed to the rapid development of the Chinese economy. But with the dramatic change of the whole economic framework, the mono-bank system could no longer adapt to the new realities. The first reforms were undertaken in 1983. The People's Bank of China (PBC) was separated into two parts: the central bank still called the PBC and the Industrial and Commercial Bank of China (ICBC) responsible for financial services of the industrial and commercial sector. Since then a new banking structure was formed in China with the PBC as the central bank on the top and four specialized banks focusing on specialized sectors at the bottom. The four specialized banks are the Agricultural Bank of China (ABC), the Industrial and Commercial Bank of China (ICBC), the People's Construction Bank of China now the China Construction Bank (CCB), and the Bank of China (BOC). At the same time non-bank financial institutions emerged to satisfy increasing needs for financial services. In the mid-1990s the commercialization of the four specialized banks had begun. The four specialized banks were transferred during the commercialization reform into the biggest four state-owned commercial banks (SOCBs), which are also called "big four" in short. In 2004 ownership reform was started aiming at restructuring the SOCBs to joint-stock commercial banks. As of 2006 the BOC, the CCB and the ICBC all had published their shares on stock markets. The ABC was the last SOCB which finished the transformation in 2009 and was listed on stock market in 2010. This symbolized a reform tendency towards gradual liberalization. More and more private and foreign financial institutions are also engaging in Chinese financial markets situated primarily in flourishing urban areas. In the urban financial markets in China, there exist diverse financial intermediates to satisfy various financial needs.

Enormous changes have also taken place in rural markets. Three significant changes can be noticed in the rural financial reform since 1979. First, the traditional specialized bank for agriculture-related services, the ABC, withdrew from the rural financial market under the county level in 1996 and became a SOCB. Since 2000, the ABC has closed 8,601 outlets in the central People's Republic of China (PRC) and 4,635 in the western PRC (Zhang et al. 2010: 24). The main business of the ABC focuses on commercial financial services in counties and cities. Second, the Agricultural Development Bank of China (ADBC) was established in 1994 to take over part of policy loan business from the ABC and the ICBC. Its loans are granted mainly to enterprises for the purchase, storage and processing of agricultural products and local governments for projects of infrastructure or public facilities. No loans of the ADBC are granted to rural households. Third, Rural Credit Cooperatives (RCCs), under the direction of the ABC since 1979, were separated from the ABC and mandated to service rural households and small rural enterprises independently in 1996. RCCs become the dominant banking institutions in the Chinese rural areas. Since 2010 some of the qualified RCCs were further reformed to rural commercial banks (RCBs) and rural cooperative banks (RcoBs). Commercialization of financial institutions is also taking place in the Chinese rural areas.

With the withdrawal of commercial banks from rural financial markets under the county level, RCCs have become the dominant financial intermediaries in rural areas. The only Rural Financial Institution (RFI) that can compete with RCCs in terms of the number of grassroots operational offices and coverage rate in rural areas is the Postal Savings Bank of China (PSBC). The PSBC began to offer lending services like microcredit loans to rural enterprises and small farmers which are mutually guaranteed by groups of farmer households from 2006. In the arena of lending services, the PSBC is still in the beginning phases and its lending volume cannot be compared with that of RCCs. The conclusion of this analysis is that in the PRC's rural institutional lending markets, RCCs remain the main suppliers of lending services and occupy an important position for the whole safety and efficiency of Chinese rural financial markets. The development of RCCs will decide the whole financial situation in Chinese rural areas.

My research primarily bears on RCCs as they are still viewed as indispensable financial entities in rural areas, and their collapse or disappearance from the rural markets will create a vacuum in the rural financial market. My analysis will unfold along the following lines:

In the first part, essential terms related to the dissertation will be defined like rural areas, agriculture-related loans and rural loans. Based on it an overall supply situation of financial services in rural areas will be depicted from the perspective of banking branch number, scale of agriculture-related loans, concentration situation of agriculture-related loans. Then the institutional structure of rural financial markets will be described. The main formal financial institutions active in rural financial markets will be introduced (e.g. the ABC, the ADBC, the PSBC and RCCs) from the perspective of their historical development, their business scale, their main rural business products and the scale of their rural loan business. At the end of this section, a horizontal comparison between these rural financial institutions (RFIs) will be made to illustrate the position of different RFIs in the Chinese rural financial market. Informal financial structures will not be considered in this dissertation.

The second part will focus on the supervisory authorities for the rural financial market and their main supervisory methods. The regulatory responsibilities of the PBC and the supervisory work of the China Banking Regulatory Commission (CBRC) will be illustrated by an introduction to their internal governance structure followed by a discussion on its methods of prudential supervision. The present introduction to the prudential supervision of the Chinese banking system is a pioneering work. I have had to carefully navigate the jungle of hundreds of supervisory policies published by the CBRC since 2003 in order to develop this thesis. The CBRC has never published any paper to summarize and present the entire framework of its supervisory methods. The only resources available are various uncategorized policies, announcements and guidelines published by it. I selected only the documents relevant to the main supervisory items and categorized them according to their themes (e.g. supervision of capital, liquidity risk, credit risk, and profitability risk). There are two reasons to include this part in the dissertation. First, standards for business-running and performance of Chinese financial institutions can be introduced in this way. Second, the supervisory methods and indicators serve as a reliable tool to evaluate the performance of financial institutions. They will be used later to evaluate the performance of RCCs.

The main body of my research work will be devoted to RCCs. This section is divided into three chapters. In this section, the performance of RCCs will be evaluated with respect to their main financial operations, performance, and the entire reform process. The thrust is to discover the obstacles that may affect the performance of RCCs such as governance weaknesses, historical burdens, government intervention credit distribution, and asset management problems and to check if the attempts at reform since 1996 have brought any positive changes in terms of the aforementioned obstacles. The reform process after 2003 will be given more attention and a few concrete case studies will further illustrate the reform process and results of the reforms.

Because of the access difficulty of Chinese literature from Germany, I've taken a lot of internet resources as reference. Most of them are from the official websites of the CBRC and the PBC or homepages of some banking institutions. The documents cited from the websites are mainly original regulations, banking institutions' annual reports, journal articles and news. So they're reliable internet sources.

Part I Financial Supply Situation and Existing Structure of Formal Banking Institutions in Rural Areas

2. Financial supply situation and existing structure of formal banking institutions in rural areas

Rural financial services are important for the development of the rural economy. In the planned economy system, significant funds were transferred from rural areas to support the growth of urban areas. The first part of this thesis will introduce the present financial supply situation and main formal banking institutions of Chinese rural areas.

The term "rural areas" refers to counties (county-level cities) and sub-county areas in China. At the end of 2011, there were 2,853 county level divisions and 40,466 township and village level divisions in China (http://baike.baidu.com/view/787783.htm).

2.1 Overall supply situation of rural banking services

By the end of 2009, there were 127,000 banking branches operating at and below the county level in China. As table 2-1 clearly shows, RCCs have the largest number of outlets at and below the county level. The number of RCCs' banking branches made up around 50% of all financial institutions at and below the county level from 2004 to 2009. Unlike other financial institutions, RCCs are independent financial entities at the county, township, and village levels. Because of the extensive autonomy of their operation, the large number of RCC branches cannot form a real network.

The PSBC takes second place in terms of the number of branches, accounting for around 20% of all branches. The PSBC's branches enjoy the advantage of belonging to one financial entity whose member branches are all electronically connected with each other.

In third place is the ABC with 10% of the market share of branches. RCCs, the PSBC and the ABC are the three dominant financial forces in the Chinese rural areas. Their total number of branches in rural areas comprises around 80% of all branches.

Table 2-1: **Number of banking branches at and below the county level from 2004 to 2009**

Institutions/Year	2004	2005	2006	2007	2009
Banking branches in total	**134,073**	**128,728**	**123,974**	**124,300**	**127,000**
RCC branches	60,869	55,953	52,089	52,000	60,325
PSBC branches	23,239	23,468	23,695	n.a.	n.a.
ABC branches	16,926	15,511	13,175	13.1	n.a.
ADBC branches	1,555	1,533	1,517	n.a.	n.a.

Source: PBC 2011: 5/Wang 2009: 19/Zhou 2009b: 34

Note: RCC branches here do not include branches of rural commercial banks (RCBs) and rural cooperative banks (RcoBs).

The coverage of these financial institutions at and below the county level is satisfactory. There were 2,853 county level divisions and 40,466 township divisions in China by the end of 2011 (http://baike.baidu.com/view/787783.htm). The number of banking branches at and below the county level sharply surpassed the number of administrative units of counties and townships. According to the PBC's report, 30 out of 31 provinces in China realized comprehensive coverage of financial services in all townships and villages by December 2010; 10 provinces realized comprehensive coverage of financial institutions in all townships and villages (PBC 2011: 5).

The current research on the financial supply situation in rural areas will focus mainly on the loan supply situation. Other financial services like deposits, remittance, settlement or agency services will not be specially considered. Agriculture-related loans are the most important indicator to illustrate the loan supply situation in Chinese rural areas. Since September 2007, Chinese financial institutions have applied the special statistical system of agriculture-related loans. In this system, data of agriculture-related loans is presented in three ways: loan purpose, loan distribution region and lending clients. Table 2-2 displays all loan items according to the three illustration methods of agriculture-related loans.

Table 2-2:   **Classification of agriculture-related loans**

Three illustration methods	Loan items
Loan purpose	1. Farming, forestry, animal husbandry, sideline production and fishery 2. Circulation of agricultural materials, farm and sideline products 3. Rural infrastructure construction 4. Processing of agricultural products 5. Agricultural means of production 6. Farmland construction 7. Agricultural technology 8. Other loans
Distribution region	1. Rural loans (1) Rural households (2) Rural enterprises and various non-business organizations 2. Agriculture-related loans extended to urban enterprises and various non-business organizations
Lending clients	1. Loans to rural households 2. Loans to enterprises (1) Rural enterprises (2) Urban enterprises 3. Loans to various non-business organizations (1) Non-business organizations in rural areas (2) Non-business organizations in urban areas

Source: PBC 2011: 3-4

Agriculture-related loans are not necessarily exclusive to rural areas. According to the loan distribution region, agriculture-related loans are divided into rural loans and loans granted to urban enterprises and various urban non-business organizations for purposes related to agriculture, rural areas and peasants (the so called Sannong). Rural loans as a sub-category of agriculture-related loans can reliably illustrate the distribution of loans to rural areas.

Table 2-3:   **Amount of outstanding agriculture-related loans of the whole banking sector from 2009 to 2012**

Unit: RMB trillion and %

Year/Items	Outstanding agriculture-related loans	Proportion to total outstanding loans in China
2009	9.14	21.5
2010	11.77	23.1
2011	14.60	25.1
2012	17.60	26.2

Source: Almanac of China's Finance and Banking 2009-2012

Table 2-3 shows the total amount of outstanding agriculture-related loans and their respective proportions to the total outstanding loans in China from 2009 to 2012. From 2009 to 2012, the total amount of agriculture-related loans increased RMB 8.46 trillion. Their proportion to the total outstanding loans of banking sector increased slightly by 4.7% (see table 2-3). Upon closer analysis, we find that 70.8% of agriculture-related loans were granted to enterprises and 22.1% were granted to rural households in 2010 (PBC 2011: 4). The amount of loans to rural households in 2010 was RMB 2.6 trillion (PBC 2011: 3). By the end of 2012 the amount of loans to rural households increased to RMB 3.6 trillion (PBC 2013d: 1). 85,240,000 rural households have acquired loans from formal financial institutions, which is over 30% of all rural households in China (CBRC 2013a).

The concentration of agriculture-related loans in all financial institutions is reflected in the data in Table 2-4. Agriculture-related loans were concentrated in three main types of financial institutions, namely SOCBs, policy banks and rural cooperative financial institutions (i.e. RCCs, RCBs and RcoBs) in 2007. The concentration level was not so high. 36.4% of agriculture-related loans in 2007 were concentrated in SOCBs and 34.1% in rural cooperative financial institutions (see table 2-4). The lower the concentration, the more diversified the rural financial market. It should be borne in mind that there is a broad spectrum of agriculture-related loans, and loans to rural households only made up 22.1% of total agriculture-related loans in 2010. If we calculate the concentration level of loans to rural households, the concentration level in rural cooperative financial institutions will be very high.

Table 2-4: **Amount and percentage of agriculture-related loans in different financial institutions (FIs) at the end of 2007**

Unit: RMB trillion and %

FIs/Items	Outstanding agriculture-related loans	Proportion to total agriculture-related loans
SOCBs	2.2282	36.4
Policy banks	1.2862	21.0
JSCBs	0.3964	6.5
City commercial banks	0.1070	1.8
Rural cooperative financial institutions	2.0850	34.1
Other FIs	0.0123	0.2
Sum	6.1151	100.0

Source: Wang 2009: 23

The tables above provide a brief overview of the most important aspects of the financial supply situation in Chinese rural areas. Main items illustrated here include total banking branch number, institutional coverage level, amount of agriculture-related loans, and concentration level of agriculture-related loans in different groups of financial institutions. We notice an increase in the number of banking branches and agriculture-related loans in recent years. The coverage level of these financial institutions is also satisfactory. The overall supply situation will be used as a reference to show the importance of each financial institution in the rural financial market.

2.2   Main formal financial entities active in rural areas

The Chinese rural financial structure is a combination of three major financial forces, namely policy, commercial and cooperative finance. These financial institutions take precedence not only in terms of their total amount of assets but also in credit offering.

New types of financial institutions are also emerging in the Chinese rural market. Microcredit companies, village and township banks (VTBs), lending companies and rural mutual credit cooperatives (RMCCs) were officially introduced as new forms of rural financial institutions in 2005. Their importance is increasing and their emergence has increased diversity and positive competition in the Chinese rural financial market.

The primary formal financial entities active in the Chinese financial market will be introduced with respect to their historical development, overall business situation, and features and scale of their rural financial services. The description aims not only at giving an overview of the supply situation of official financial services but also at identifying their business difference between these entities and ascertaining the position of RCCs among all the formal financial suppliers.

Figure 2-1: Structural diagram of the system of rural formal financial organizations in China

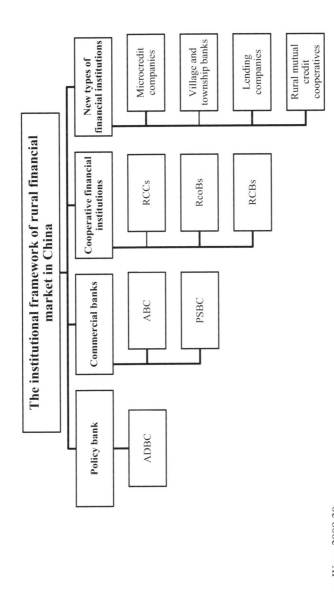

2.2.1 Agricultural Bank of China

The Agricultural Bank of China (ABC) is one of the four largest joint-stock commercial banks in China. It has a long history of running business in rural areas. In 1951, the Agricultural Cooperative Bank--the predecessor of the ABC--was established. It functioned initially as a specialized subsidiary unit of the PBC and existed only for a year (ABC 2012b: 22). The financial institution known as the ABC was twice established in 1955 and 1963, but both manifestations were very short-lived and it functioned more as a branch of the PBC in the mono-bank system.

With the breakdown of mono-bank system in 1979, the ABC was resurrected as a specialized bank along with other specialized banks (i.e. BOC, ICBC and CCB). The ABC was made responsible for the management of agricultural funding, offering rural credit in a centralized manner and managing RCCs. In ABC's specialized bank period from 1979 to 1993, it financed the development of agricultural resources and farming technology, helped establish key national production bases and supported export-oriented township enterprises with its loan services (ABC 2012b: 20). In the mid-1980s, more than 98% of its loans were granted to rural areas (ABC 2012b: 20).

Figure 2-2:   **Four development phases of the ABC from 1951 to present**

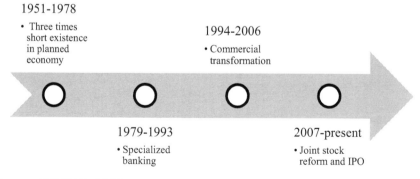

Source: ABC 2012b: 20-21

In December 1993, the State Council published the "Decision of the State Council on reform of the financial system". According to the decision, specialized banks should be reformed as state-owned commercial-oriented banks. The ABC followed the requirements and enlarged its business to urban areas. Accordingly, part of ABCs' policy related banking was transferred to the newly established ADBC in 1994. In 1996 according to the requirements of the State Council's "Decision on rural financial system reform" the administrative relationship between the ABC and RCCs was severed. RCCs became independent FIs separated from ABC's management. In July 2000, ABC's non-performing assets were transferred to the China Great Wall Asset Management Company (AMC), which significantly reduced ABC's non-performing loan ratio (NPL ratio) and boosted its capital adequacy ratio (CAR) so that the ABC could improve its balance sheet before commercialization (PBC 2012b: 21). In the commercial transformation period from 1993 to 2006, the ABC gradually shifted its business from rural to urban areas. Since the late 1990s, the ABC has withdrawn 21,000 branches from rural areas (Wang 2009: 102).

On January 19, 2007, the third National Financial Conference proposed that the ABC should undertake joint stock reform and defined reform principle as "orienting towards Sannong business, undertaking an overall restructuring, operating commercially and going public at an appropriate time" (ABC 2012b: 23). In 2008, the China's State Council formally approved the joint stock reform plan of the ABC. In October 2008, Central Huijin Investment Ltd. injected RMB 130 billion into the capital base of the ABC. With the existing RMB 130 billion capital held by the Ministry of Finance, the core capital of the ABC reached RMB 260 billion (PBC 2011: 11-12). On December 1st of the same year, the ABC completed the removal of RMB 815.7 billion of bad assets (PBC 2011: 12). The precondition of joint stock reform has been fulfilled. On January 15, 2009, Agricultural Bank of China Limited was finally established with the mandate of "strengthening Sannong banking businesses, serving both urban and county areas, maximizing shareholders returns, and assisting staff development" (ABC 2012b: 10). Two shareholders of ABC were Central Huijin Investment Ltd and the Ministry of Finance, each with a 50% stake (Marks 2010: 23). On July 15 and 16, 2010, the Agricultural Bank of China Limited was listed on the Shanghai Stock Exchange and the Hong Kong Stock Exchange respectively. This event marked the completion of a historical transformation from an exclusively state-owned commercial bank to a public joint-stock commercial bank, the latest among the "big four" SOCBs (PBC 2011: 12).

The ABC is the oldest and largest in terms of assets of all rural financial institutions. By the end of 2012, the asset volume of the ABC reached RMB 13.244 trillion (ABC 2013a: 12), ranking as the third largest bank in China in terms of asset volume behind ICBC and CCB in 2012. It possessed 23,472 domestic branches, 9 overseas branches and 12 domestic and overseas holding companies by the end of 2012 (ABC 2013a: 14). The data in Table 2-5 demonstrates that the profitability of the ABC is high and increasingly stable. The assets of the ABC also show good quality with a very low NPL ratio of 1.33% by the end of 2012 (Table 2-5).

Table 2-5:   Bank balance sheet of the ABC from 2002 to 2012

Unit: RMB billion and %

Year/ Items	Asset volume	Outstanding deposit	Outstanding loans	Net profit	Return on assets	NPL ratio
2002	2976.566	2479.618	1912.960	10.940	0.37	n.a.
2003	3494.016	2997.288	2268.393	19.641	0.56	30.66
2004	4013.769	3491.549	2590.072	31.974	0.80	26.73
2005	4771.019	4036.854	2829.291	42.483	0.89	26.17
2006	5343.943	4730.372	3139.431	58.157	1.09	23.43
2007	5305.506	5287.194	3480.105	43.787	0.88	23.57
2008	7014.351	6097.428	3100.159	51.474	0.84	4.32
2009	8882.588	7497.618	4138.187	65.002	0.82	2.91
2010	10337.406	8887.905	4956.741	94.907	0.99	2.03
2011	11677.577	9622.026	5628.705	121.960	1.11	1.55
2012	13244.324	10862.935	6433.399	145.131	1.16	1.33

Source: ABC Annual Report 2004-2012

By the end of 2012, there were 12,669 branches of 23,472 ABC branches nationwide located at and below the county level-- 56.3% of all ABC branches (ABC 2013a: 13). A special division known as the County Area Banking Division has been established since March 2008 at each level of ABC branches to be responsible for the management of county area banking business. The vertical organizational structure of the County Areas Banking Division management system is described in Figure 2-3. This division has its own balance sheet and is separated from the ABC. Business of the ABC in country areas includes services for deposits, loans, debit and credit cards, settlements, new rural pension and insurance and new rural cooperative medical insurance (ABC 2012b: 47). By the end of 2012, 127.82 billion "Huinong" debit cards have been issued, and the number of county branches providing new rural pension and insurance services and new rural cooperative medical insurance has increased to 1,532 counties (ABC 2013a: 31).

Figure 2-3:   Organizational structure of ABC's County Areas Banking Division management system

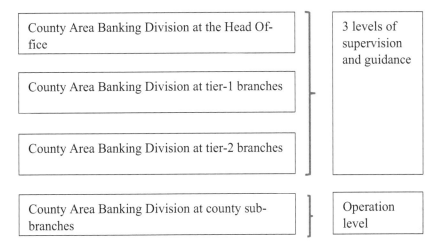

Source: ABC 2012a: 66

The ABC provided 103 special products for county areas and 413 banking products for urban and county areas by the end of 2012(ABC 2013b: 62). Corporate loan products comprise loans to leading agricultural industrialization enterprises, county area SME loans, county area urbanization loans and loans for county area merchandise distribution (ABC 2010: 54). Agriculture-related personal products include microcredit loans to rural households, private business loans to rural households and loans for house construction of farmers in earthquake-stricken areas (http://www.abchina. com/en/agro-related-business/). Some products are designed to take regional condition into consideration (e.g. guaranteed loans to rural households secured by forestry rights, operating rights over land or operating rights over residential houses; guaranteed loans to SMEs secured by their characteristic agricultural products) (ABC 2012a: 66). The amount of loans to the agricultural industry and agriculture-related loans from the ABC between 2006 and 2012 is shown in Table 2-6. The proportion of agriculture-related loans to the total outstanding loans of the ABC has decreased from 54.15% in 2006 to 29.76% in 2012, though the total amount of agriculture-related loans increased steadily from 2008 to 2012 (see Table 2-6).

By the end of 2012, the ABC's balance of agriculture-related loans had increased to RMB 1.9144 trillion (ABC 2013a: 29). This amount is the second largest of all financial institutions active in rural areas, just behind the amount of agriculture-related loans issued by RCCs. RMB 1.467 trillion in loans were extended to national and provincial agricultural industrialization leading enterprises (ABC 2013b: 34). Only RMB 132.77 billion in loans were extended to rural households, which cannot be compared with rural cooperative financial institutions (see Table 2-6). In 2010, the outstanding balance of loans to rural households of RCCs, RcoBs and RCBs amounted to RMB 2 trillion (PBC 2011: 70).

Table 2-6: **Balance of ABC agriculture-related loans from 2006 to 2012**

Unit: RMB billion and %

Year/Items	Outstanding agriculture-related loans	Proportion of agriculture-related loans	Loans to rural households	Loans for rural urbanization	Loans for small and micro enterprises
2006	1700.000	54.15	n.a.	n.a.	n.a.
2007	1209.500	34.75	n.a.	n.a.	n.a.
2008	933.000	30.10	99.80	n.a.	n.a.
2009	1193.413	28.84	68.00	27.343	376.576
2010	1473.700	29.66	107.30	55.159	461.081
2011	1675.300	29.76	130.60	76.432	575.219
2012	1914.400	29.76	132.77	70.000	599.801

Source: ABC Annual report 2006-2012/ABC corporate social responsibility report 2011-2012

Generally speaking, the ABC still holds its place as a very important rural financial supplier with a large scale of agriculture-related loans. Furthermore, the ABC has a lot of experiences in the rural lending business. The focus of the ABC's loan business in rural areas is serving leading agricultural industrialization enterprises. This is a safe and profitable service model that can satisfy the task mandated for the ABC of serving urban and county areas and maximizing shareholders returns.

2.2.2 Agricultural Development Bank of China

The Agricultural Development Bank of China (ADBC) is a state-owned policy bank under the direct administration of the State Council. It was established in 1994 with a head office in Beijing. In the same year, several policy banks including the China Development Bank and the Export-Import Bank of China were established. The three policy banks were set up following the "Decision of the State Council on reform of the financial system" published in December 1993 aimed at freeing the former state-owned specialized banks from the responsibility of disbursing government-directed loans. The ADBC processes RMB 20 billion of registered capital (ADBC 2013: 1). By the end of 2012 the ADBC had accumulated RMB 2293.079 billion in total assets (ADBC 2013: 1). The whole institutional structure of the ADBC consisted of one head office in Beijing, 31 branches of provinces, autonomous regions and municipalities, 303 prefecture-level branches and 1,670 sub-branches and offices at the county level (ADBC 2013: 21). There were no branches set up under the county level.

The main tasks of the ADBC at the beginning of its establishment included the management of funds for purchasing grain, cotton and edible oil and distribution of loans for integrated agricultural development and poverty alleviation. With the granted loans for purchasing grain, cotton and edible oil, the food safety of the State should be guaranteed. These loan services were taken over from the ABC and the ICBC. In 1994, RMB 259.2 billion policy loans were transferred from the ABC and the ICBC to the ADBC (ADBC 2005a). In March 1998, the State Council decided to transfer businesses related to poverty alleviation, comprehensive agricultural development and sideline business of grain and cotton enterprises from the ADBC to SOCBs (ADBC 2005a). The ADBC was required to concentrate on the management of funds for purchasing grain, cotton and edible oil only (ADBC 2005a).

After 2004, the ADBC began to expand its business. In the first step of its expansion, it broadened its client base from traditional state-owned grain, cotton and edible oil enterprises to include enterprises with multiple-ownership in accordance with the State Council's decision on the marketing reform of grain (ADBC 2005a). It added new business such as loans for agricultural flagship enterprises and agricultural processing enterprises, loans for agricultural science and technology and loans for the construction of rural infrastructure, agricultural integrated development and means of production to its business structure (ADBC 2005a). Table 2-7 summarizes the loan business of the ADBC.

Table 2-7:   **Loan business of the ADBC at present**

Loans for the purchase, reserve and distribution of grain, cotton and edible oils;	
Loans for the special reserve of meat, sugar, tobacco, wool and chemical fertilizer;	
Loans for leading industrial enterprises in agriculture, forestry, animal husbandry, side-line products and fishery sectors, as well as in grain, cotton and edible oil processing;	
Loans for the purchase of grain, cotton and oil plant seeds;	
Loans for the upgrade of grain storage facilities and the technical innovation of cotton enterprises;	
Loans in support of small agricultural enterprises, and agricultural science and technology projects;	
Loans in support of the construction of rural infrastructure projects	Including roads, power grids, water supply systems (including drinking water projects), and information networks (postal service and telecommunications), as well as energy and environmental facilities in rural areas;
Loans in support of integrated agricultural development projects	Including the development and upgrade of farmland irrigation and water conservancy systems, and the development and construction of agricultural production bases, agriculture eco-environmental projects, agricultural technology service systems and rural circulation systems;

Continuation
Table 2-7: **Loan business of the ADBC at present**

Loans in support of the urbanization development of counties	Including urban infrastructure projects, cultural, education, health, environmental facilities, commercial facilities for local citizens, and the renovation of concentrated housing projects for farmers (including concentrated dwelling districts, squatter settlements and mud thatched cottages in rural areas);
Loans for the supply of agricultural input in the field of their circulation and distribution	

Source: ADBC 2013: 3

The ADBC has described its business structure as "one body with two wings." In this metaphor, grain, cotton and edible oil credit represents the main body, while agriculture industrialization and medium and long-term agricultural and rural credits make up the two wings (ADBC 2005a). The loan product design of the ADBC shows a robust policy character. It incorporates crucial services such as: loans for the purchase of essential agricultural products to maintain food safety, loans for the construction of infrastructure projects to improve rural infrastructure, loans for the development of counties to improve the public facilities of rural areas and accelerate urbanization. No loans are granted to rural households. All these loans should be counted in the category of agriculture-related loans. The outstanding loans of the ADBC in 2012 made up 12.4% of all agriculture-related loans in China.

The concrete loan and deposit scale of the ADBC from 2004 to 2012 is shown in Figure 2-4. The total loans of the ADBC reached RMB 2.1844 trillion, while the outstanding deposits amounted to only RMB 422.05 billion by the end of 2012. It is obvious that the ADBC's deposits were insufficient to meet necessary services. The ADBC is not allowed to provide deposit services to the public, and this fact is responsible for the ADBC's deposit deficit. Only enterprises and institutions which maintain accounts with the ADBC are allowed to deposit funds. The ADBC has other funding channels like issuance of financial bonds, borrowing from the PBC, inter-bank deposits, oversees funds, etc.. Among these, bond issuance is the primary contributor supplemented by corporate deposits and inter-bank loans (ADBC 2005b).

Figure 2-4:   Balance of loans and deposits of the ADBC from 2004 to 2012

Unit: RMB billion

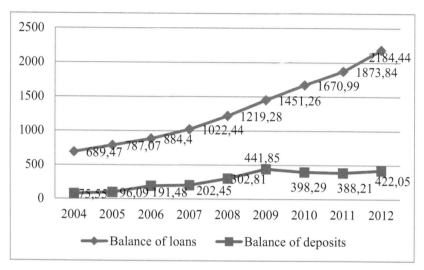

Source: ADBC 2013

Overall speaking, the ADBC plays an important role in offering policy financial services for the Chinese rural areas. Loans are granted mainly to enterprises for the purchase, storage and processing of agricultural products and local governments for projects of infrastructure or public facilities. Rural households and rural enterprises of other sectors are not the clients of the ADBC.

2.2.3 Postal Savings Bank of China

The Postal Savings Bank Ltd. Co. of China (PSBC) was officially established as a commercial bank in 2007. Before its establishment, the PSBC had existed since January 1986 as a part of the China Post system in the form of postal savings offices when the Ministry of Posts and Telecommunications (now the Ministry of Industry and Information Technology) and the PBC announced the intention of launching a postal savings business in post offices (Zhang et al. 2010: 20). This proposal was tested in 12 pilot cities and then implemented nationwide in March 1986. From 1986 to 1990, post savings offices functioned as agents designated by the PBC to operate postal savings business and transfer the collected savings to the PBC earning 0.22% commission compounded monthly of their current outstanding deposits in the PBC (Zhang et al. 2010: 20). The PBC also paid interest on postal savings in addition to the 0.22% commission (Zhang et al. 2010: 20). In 1990, the postal savings business became the postal savings offices' own business. But the collected savings still needed to be deposited at the PBC in the one common account shared by all postal savings offices. Interest rate for postal savings at the PBC was 4.13%, which was on average more than 2% higher than the interest rate of deposits from commercial banks in the PBC (Zhang et al. 2010: 20). Through this method, large amount of funds was transferred from rural areas to the central bank; the PBC then reallocated them for industrialization in urban areas.

In August 2003, postal savings offices were authorized to independently utilize new savings at its own discretion and promote commercial viability of postal savings. The favorable re-depositing conditions in the PBC were also rescinded and already deposited funds in the PBC were returned to postal savings offices over the five consecutive years from August 2005 (Zhang et al. 2010: 29). In this period, postal savings offices used their savings to do some asset-related businesses like negotiated deposits and investments on bonds. Lending business was not opened at postal savings offices until March 2006 when the system of micro credit backed by time deposit certificates was first piloted in Fujian Province.

On December 31, 2006, the CBRC approved the incorporation of the PSBC and permitted the China Post Group to become the sole investor of the PSBC. In March 2007, the PSBC was officially established as the fifth largest commercial bank in the PRC under the supervision of the PBC and the CBRC. In January 2012, the PSBC was further converted into a company limited by shares from a former limited liability company (China Post Group 2012: 34). The PSBC defined itself as a large retail commercial bank (China Post Group 2013). The mandate of the PSBC is to provide services to "farming, farmers and the rural community", small- and medium-sized enterprises and urban and rural residents; to use postal network advantages, to reinforce its internal control and to run its business in a manner of compliance and stability (China Post Group 2012: 34).

According to the latest data, the volume of PSBC's assets is over RMB 4.7 trillion according to the newest data on the website of the PSBC, the sixth largest in the Chinese banking sector (PSBC 2013b). Its latest outstanding deposit reached RMB 4.5 trillion, the fifth largest in the Chinese banking sector (PSBC 2013b). Only the "big four" possess more outstanding deposits than the PSBC. However, the PSBC's most important advantage is its savings network covering urban and rural areas. By the end of October 2012, the number of interconnected postal savings outlets exceeded 39,000 (PSBC 2013b). Among them, approximately 27,000 postal savings outlets are located at and below the county level and made up 71% of all PSBC branches (PSBC 2013a: 1). More than 50% of the postal savings outlets are located below the county level according to the data of the PSBC outlet distribution in 2008 (China Post Group 2009: 36). This distribution advantage makes the PSBC very suitable to provide financial services in rural areas.

Table 2-8:   **Main balance sheet data of the PSBC from 2007 to 2011**

Unit: RMB billion and %

Year/Items	Assets	Outstanding deposits	Outstanding loans	NPL ratio	CAR
2007	1060.000	1721.700	109.983	n.a.	n.a.
2008	1354.414	2080.000	261.403	n.a.	n.a.
2009	2704.512	2405.000	409.464	0.19	8.04
2010	3396.820	3259.701	544.276	0.25	n.a.
2011	4120.000	3936.600	660.900	0.57	n.a.

Source: China Post Group annual report 2007-2011

The most important and incidentally the most traditional services offered by the PSBC are deposit and remittance services. The PSBC's network for remittance services is even larger than that for its deposit services. By the end of 2010, 45,000 PSBC outlets offered remittance services (China Post Group 2011: 32). The PSBC has played an indispensable role in offering remittance services. RMB 1499.348 billion have been remitted by PSBC as of the end of 2010 (China Post Group 2011: 33).

The PSBC's loan service business is still in the beginning phase. Since the PSBC's establishment in 2007, it has been qualified to offer asset business like other commercial banks. The range of PSBC's asset business has enlarged from negotiated deposits, bonds investment and inter-bank lending to include short- and long-term loans. Representative loan services include loans pledged with time deposit certificates and microcredit loans. Because the loan services have only been available for 7 years, the NPL ratio is very low (see Table 2-8).

By the end of 2011, the PSBC had dispensed RMB 135.367 billion agriculture-related loans, constituting 20.5% of outstanding loans of the PSBC in 2011 (PSBC 2013a: 1). In 2012, the agriculture-related loans of the PSBC increased further to RMB 187.815 billion (PSBC 2013a: 1). Around 2.2 million households have benefited from loans supplied by the PSBC (PSBC 2013a: 10). Loans offered by the PSBC are small. The average value of each agriculture-related loan reached RMB 90,000 by the end of 2012 (PSBC 2013a: 10). The most important loan service in rural areas is micro credit. The average value of microcredit loans was RMB 60,000 by the end of 2012 (PSBC 2013a: 10). By the end of 2010, the accumulated total of loans pledged with time deposit certificates reached RMB 55.854 billion, while the accumulated total of microcredit loans dispensed at and below the county level was RMB 188.503 billion (PBC 2011: 13).

The PSBC is an important financial institution in rural areas offering deposit, remittance and agency services. While its loan service team is still being built, the PSBC has great room for development in offering loan services in rural areas on account of its abundant deposits and large number of rural outlets.

2.2.4 Rural cooperative financial institutions

Rural cooperative financial institutions are independent and dispersed cooperative financial institutions active in rural areas that include Rural Credit Cooperatives (RCCs), Rural Commercial Banks (RCBs) and Rural Cooperative Banks (RcoBs). They are the backbone of the rural financial market because of their large coverage and long history dating back to 1951 as financial institutions in rural areas. According to the newest data, there were altogether 49,034 RCC branches, 19,910 RCB branches and 5,463 RcoB branches in Chinese rural areas by the end of 2012 with a total of 74,707 branches in 2012, the highest in comparison with other rural financial institutions (PBC 2013d: 2). These branches, however, did not belong to one legal entity. RCCs can be set up either at the county level or at the township and village levels. RCBs and RcoBs exist as county-level legal entities. By the end of 2012, there were 1,927 RCC legal entities, 337 RCB legal entities and 147 RcoB legal entities (PBC 2013d: 2). The reason that RCCs, RCBs and RcoBs are placed together is because before the commercialization reform of RCCs piloted in 2000 there were no RCBs and RcoBs in rural areas, whereas after the reform, qualified RCCs merged together to form RCBs and RcoBs. Some RCCs chose to join together at the county level to become unified county RCCs. Hence, unified county RCCs, RCBs and RcoBs are originally RCC organizations.

Table 2-9:   **Asset volume of RCCs, RcoBs and RCBs from 2009 to 2011**

Unit: RMB billion

Year/Institutions	RCCs	RcoBs	RCBs	**Total**
2009	5494.5	1279.1	1866.1	**8639.7**
2010	6391.1	1500.2	2767.0	**10658.3**
2011	7204.7	1402.5	4252.7	**12859.9**
2012	7953.5	1283.5	6275.1	**15512.1**

Source: CBRC 2012a: 119/CBRC 2013b: 164

RCCs here are in essence cooperative financial institutions. Most of their shareholders are rural households and rural enterprises. Members of RCCs can invest a fixed amount to acquire membership. For unified county RCCs, the amount for natural person shareholders should not be less than RMB 1,000, and for legal person shareholders it should not be less than RMB 10,000. Members of RCCs have priority in obtaining services from RCCs and enjoy a position of preference. RCBs have abandoned the co-operative nature and are commercial oriented banks to serve financial needs in rural areas. RcoBs are transitional forms between RCBs and RCCs. They keep the qualification shares for their membership and also serve members with favorable conditions.

Table 2-10: Amount of agriculture-related loans of rural cooperative financial institutions from 2007 to 2012

Unit: RMB billion and %

Year/Items	Agriculture-related loans	Proportion to their out-standing loans	Rural loans	Loans to ru-ral house-holds
2007	2084.995	66.49	1890.285	1165.492
2008	2453.137	65.84	2222.541	1331.895
2009	3091.866	65.81	2807.709	1641.395
2010	3874.318	65.59	n.a.	2000.000
2012	5300.000	n.a.	n.a.	2700.000

Source: PBC 2011: 70/CBRC 2013a

Services provided by RCCs, RcoBs and RCBs include deposits, loans, and settlements. The highest lending rate of RCCs is 2.3 times the benchmark lending interest rate set by the PBC (PBC 2011: 41). By the end of 2010, RCC outstanding loans reached RMB 5.9 trillion, which is also the largest amount of outstanding loans among all financial institutions active in Chinese rural areas (PBC 2011: 9). Among them RMB 3.847 trillion were agriculture-related loans, while the agriculture-related loans from the ABC amounted to RMB 1.47 trillion, from the ADBC RMB 1.67 trillion in the same period. Out of the RMB 5.9 trillion in loans, RMB 2 trillion were granted to rural households (see table 2-10). By the end of 2009, 82.42 million rural households were financed by RCC loans, which covered 33.5% of all rural households (PBC 2011: 70). This suffices to prove that RCCs, RCBs and RcoBs are the main financial institutions serving financial needs in rural areas.

Figure 2-5:   Coverage of loans to rural households from rural cooperative financial institutions from 2002 to 2009

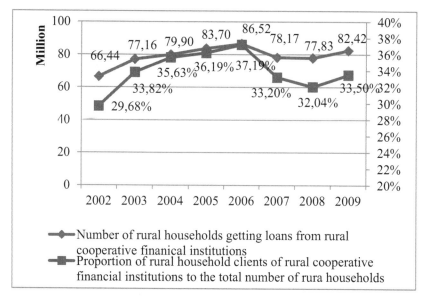

Source: PBC 2011: 70

2.2.5 New types of rural financial institutions

In China, the liberalization of the rural financial market began with the pilot reform program launched by the PBC to introduce microcredit companies in the five counties of Guizhou Province, Inner Mongolia Autonomous Region, Shaanxi Province, Shanxi Province, and Sichuan Province in the second half of 2005 (Zhang et al. 2010: 29).

Figure 2-6:   Pilot provinces of microcredit companies in 2005

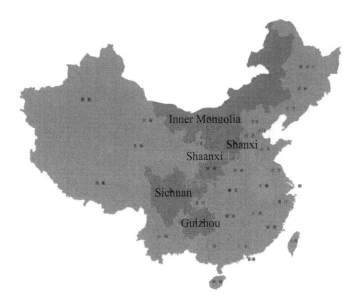

Further step towards diversification of rural financial institutions followed in December 2006. The CBRC relaxed market-entry requirements on financial institutions and piloted the liberalization of rural financial market in Gansu, Hebei, Jilin, Qinghai, Sichuan provinces and Inner Mongolia Autonomous Region (Zhang et al. 2010: 30). This time, three new types of rural financial institutions were permitted to be set up in rural areas: village and township banks (VTBs), rural mutual credit cooperatives (RMCCs), and lending companies. In January 2007, a range of regulations about the management and supervision for the three new types of rural financial institutions were published by the CBRC, which marked the official opening of the rural financial market nationwide.

In the past six years, these new types of financial institutions have experienced quick development especially microcredit companies and VTBs. By the end of 2012, there were 6,080 microcredit companies and 800 VTBs with 1,426 branches nationwide established (see Table 2-11). The outstanding loans of microcredit companies reached RMB 592.1 billion, a number which stands to rival the total outstanding loans of the PSBC (see Table 2-11). VTBs' outstanding loans amounted to RMB 233 billion. The number of lending companies and RMCCs, on the other hand, is still comparatively low.

Table 2-11:   Information of new financial institutions in rural areas by the end of 2012

FIs/Itmes	Number of legal entities	Number of branches	Assets (RMB hillion)	Outstanding loans (RMB billion)
Microcredit companies	6080	n.a.	514.7	592.1
VTBs	800	1426	434.3	233.0
Lending com-panies	14	14	n.a.	n.a.
RMCCs	49	49	n.a.	n.a.

Source: PBC 2013a / PBC 2013d: 2/Shenzhen Microfinance Industry Association 2013

The services offered by these new FIs are mainly loan services. VTBs are the only financial institutions allowed to take deposits from the public. RMCCs, conversely, can absorb savings from their members. Loans extended by these RFIs should be small. The interest rates of their loans are not capped. 70% of loans granted by microcredit companies should be used for rural areas, agriculture or peasants (Zhou 2009b: 36). VTBs, lending companies and RMCCs have the mandate to serve financial needs of local farmers, agricultural production and the rural economy (CBRC 2007h/i/j). According to the report of the PBC, more than 80% of the loans of TVBs, lending companies and RMCCs were extended to agriculture-related projects and SMEs (PBC 2011: 15).

The emergence of these new financial institutions has increased competition in the rural financial market and provides more financial possibilities for rural households and enterprises. This contributes in great measure to the commercialization of the rural financial market, which is good news for rural residents and rural enterprises. The rapid development brings with it a number of concerns. One shortcoming of these financial institutions is that they offer almost identical loan products. Most of their profits were earned from their lending businesses, which will make them vulnerable to any changes in the market. They may bring vitality to the market but also instability. Because most of them apart from VTBs do not offer deposit services, their influence to the public will be inevitably limited in scope. In comparison with other financial institutions, new types of financial institutions have the advantage of flexibility and a less cumbersome approval process for loan applications.

2.3   Summary

From the description above we can see enormous changes taking place in the Chinese rural financial market in the last 60 years. In the planned economy (1949-1978) there was only one formal financial entity, namely RCCs in rural areas. The ABC existed only for a short time before 1979 to provide financial services for rural areas. Now rural financial market has relatively differentiated financial institutions. The ABC and the PSBC are both large-scaled joint-stock commercial banks. The ADBC is a state-owned policy bank. RCCs, RCBs and RcoBs belong to rural cooperative financial institutions. New financial institutions like microcredit companies, VTBs, lending companies and RMCCs are partly non-bank financial institutions and partly small grassroots banks. The increase of financial institutions will bring positive competition and offer more financial possibilities for rural residents.

After introducing the situation of banking institutions separately, an overall comparison among them will be made. Table 2-12 summarizes the main agriculture-related data about the above mentioned financial institutions. From the data we can see that rural cooperative financial institutions have the largest number of branches in county areas. The number of branches of RCCs, RCBs and RcoBs is six-fold of that of the ABC and more than two and a half that of the branch number of PSBC.

In terms of assets the ABC is the financial institution with the second largest scale of assets in 2010. Rural cooperative financial institutions' total assets exceeded the assets of the ABC slightly. The asset scale of the ADBC and the PSBC cannot compare with that of ABC and rural cooperative financial institutions.

Table 2-12: **Business comparison of main rural financial institutions in 2010 and county branch number in 2012**

Items/Institutions	ABC	ADBC	PSBC	Cooperative RFIs
Branch number at the county level (2012)	12,669	1,670	27,000	74,707
Assets (2010) RMB billion	10337.4	1750.8	3396.8	10658.3
Outstanding agriculture-related loans (2010) RMB billion	1473.7	1671.0	135.4 In 2011	3870.0
Outstanding loans to rural households (2010) RMB billion	299.1	0	n.a.	2000.0

Source: CBRC 2012a: 119/PBC 2011: 9/11/12/ABC 2013a: 13/ADBC 2013: 21/PBC 2013d: 2

Furthermore, in terms of agriculture-related loans and outstanding loans for rural households, rural cooperative financial institutions held absolute the first place with the volume of agriculture-related loans of RMB 3.87 trillion (see Table 2-12). The ABDC and the ABC possessed the second and third largest amount of outstanding agriculture-related loans. From the perspective of loans to rural households, rural cooperate financial institutions are the main suppliers of loans to rural households with the outstanding volume of RMB 2 trillion. In 2010, the total outstanding loans to rural households amounted to RMB 2.6 trillion (PBC 2011: 3).

From this comparison we can conclude that rural cooperative financial institutions are undeniable the most important supplier of rural financial services at lowest administrative level. The further development direction of RCCs will directly influence financial supply situation in rural areas.

Part II   Supervisory System of the Chinese Banking Sector

3. Supervisory system of the Chinese banking sector

The financial regulatory and supervisory authorities are important actors and coordinators in financial markets. Their job consists in ensuring the safety and stability of the banking sector. They also make up the executive part of the prudential regulation system, one of the two main mechanisms by which public authorities intervene in the activity of the banking sector in addition to financial safety nets composed of deposit insurance systems and emergency liquidity assistance provided by the central bank (Rochet 2008: 1).

In China, the main regulatory and supervisory authorities in the banking sector are the PBC and the China Banking Regulatory Commission (CBRC). The PBC is responsible for regulating the banking activities and conducting the supervision at the macro-level, whereas the CBRC monitors the activities and performance of banks, closes banks that do not meet these regulations and monitors financial risk mainly at the micro-level. The importance of regulatory and supervisory authorities cannot be understated. Here the supervisory circumstances of the Chinese banking sector will be outlined: first, I will give a brief introduction to the two main supervisory authorities; second, I will detail the evaluation and supervisory indicators used by the CBRC, categorize them according to the objective of supervision and illustrate the position of different FIs and the whole banking sector measured through these indicators. The intention of including this part in the dissertation is not to introduce the supervisory work of the CBRC but to clarify the policy environment of Chinese financial markets, introduce basic China-specific banking regulations like the loan classification method, and systematically outline the supervisory framework applied in China. The introduced supervisory indicators will be used later to evaluate the performance of RCCs.

3.1   Supervisory authorities in Chinese rural financial markets

The Chinese financial sector is regulated and supervised by one central bank (i.e. the PBC) and three commissions (i.e. the CBRC, the China Insurance Regulatory Commission (CIRC) and the China Securities Regulatory Commission (CSRC)). The three commissions are responsible for the regulation and supervision of the daily performance of actors in the banking, insurance and securities markets in China. Among them, only the PBC and the CBRC are coextensive authorities in their role in the banking sector.

As the Chinese central bank, the PBC is responsible for the formulation and implementation of monetary policy with the mission to ensure the stability of the financial system. The PBC also has the duty to coordinate the three commissions and hold a quarterly joint conference to facilitate communication between them (Figure 3-1). It plays the role of a regulator in the Chinese financial market, but also at the macro-level a supervisor. Before the establishment of special commissions for the supervisory work of different financial markets, the PBC also supervised and monitored all finance-related entities and markets.

Figure 3-1:   Domestic financial regulators in China and year of their establishment

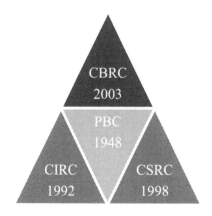

Source: ICRF 2010: 7

Established in 2003, the CBRC is authorized by the State Council to regulate the banking sector of the PRC with an exception for the territories of

Hong Kong and Macau. Before the establishment of the CBRC, the PBC was mandated to supervise all the enterprises related with the banking sector. With the establishment of the CBRC, the supervision work can eventually be separated from regulation authorities so that the supervisory authority can operate independently. The independence of the supervisory work is also guaranteed through the "Law of the People's Republic of China on banking regulation and supervision" which states that "the banking regulatory authority and its supervisory staff shall be protected by law while performing supervisory responsibilities in accordance with laws and regulations. There shall be no interference by local governments, government departments at various levels, public organizations or individuals" in article 6 (CBRC 2003d).

3.1.1 The supervisory work of the PBC

The People's Bank of China (PBC) is the central bank of China. In addition to the PBC's position as the central bank, it also functions as an administration with ministerial rank working under the leadership of the State Council (Cousin 2011: 21). Big decisions made by the PBC concerning the annual money supply, interest rates and exchange rates must be reported to and approved by the State Council (PBC 2003a). The governor of the PBC is appointed or removed by the President of the People's Republic of China (PBC 2003a). The candidate for the governor of the PBC is nominated by the Premier of the State Council and approved by the National People's Congress (PBC 2003a). The current governor of the PBC is Xiaochuan Zhou.

This big organization possesses one head office in Beijing and 36 regional offices all over China. The head office comprises altogether 18 functional departments (PBC unknown b). The main functional departments of the PBC include the Monetary Policy Department, the Financial Market Department, the Financial Stability Bureau, the Financial Survey and Statistics Department, the Accounting and Treasury Department, the Payment System Department, the Currency, Gold and Silver Bureau, the State Treasury Bureau and so on (PBC unknown b).

The legal foundation of PBC's regulatory work is the "Law on People's Bank of China" published in 1995. The "Law on the People's Bank of

China" was revised in 2003 after the establishment of the CBRC. This law regulates the main functions of the PBC, which include:

"Drafting and enforcing relevant laws, rules and regulations that are related to fulfilling its functions;

Formulating and implementing monetary policy in accordance with law;

Issuing the RMB and administering its circulation;

Regulating financial markets, including the inter-bank lending market, the inter-bank bond market, foreign exchange market and gold market;

Preventing and mitigating systemic financial risks to safeguard financial stability;

Maintaining the RMB exchange rate at adaptive and equilibrium level; Holding and managing the state foreign exchange and gold reserves;

Managing the State treasury as fiscal agent;

Making payment and settlement rules in collaboration with relevant departments and ensuring normal operation of the payment and settlement systems;

Providing guidance to anti-money laundering work in the financial sector and monitoring money-laundering related suspicious fund movement;

Developing statistics system for the financial industry and responsible for the consolidation of financial statistics as well as the conduct of economic analysis and forecast;

Administering credit reporting industry in China and promoting the building up of credit information system;

Participating in international financial activities at the capacity of the central bank;

Engaging in financial business operations in line with relevant rules;

Performing other functions prescribed by the State Council." (PBC 2003a)

The supervisory work of the PBC over the financial market has changed after the establishment of the CBRC. This change also reflected in the revised "Law on People's Bank of China", which redefined PBC's responsibilities in terms of supervision of financial market. The PBC cannot conduct direct supervision over financial institutions except some PBC related business such as implementation of deposit reserve, usage of PBC's special loans, management of RMB, foreign exchanges and gold, implementation of settlement rules, implementation of anti-money laundering rules and so on (PBC 2003a). But as a central bank it has the responsibility to stabilize financial markets and resolve financial crises. So the PBC also conducts supervisory work but in the macroeconomic sense (e.g. the supervision of financial markets, assessment of systemic risks to prevent and resolve cross-market risks and systemic financial risks) in contrast with the CBRC which concentrates on the supervision of the performance of financial institutions at the micro-level.

3.1.2 The supervisory work of the CBRC

The central government set up the CBRC to supervise the banking sector in March 2003 so that the central bank could be freed from the supervision work and supervisory independence could be achieved. The CBRC works directly under the leadership of the State Council. It has one head office in Beijing and 36 regional offices to implement policies prescribed by the head office at the provincial level (ICFR 2010:8). The location of local offices is described in Figure 3-2. The chairman of the agency now is Fulin Shang who replaced the first chairman Mingkang Liu in 2011.

Figure 3-2: **Regional offices of CBRC in China**

Source: http://www.cbrc.gov.cn/showoffices.do[15.4.2012]

The CBCR is in charge of the supervisory work of almost all financial institutions in China. As of the end of 2010 there were 3 policy banks, 5 large commercial banks, 12 joint-stock commercial banks, 147 commercial banks, 40 locally incorporated foreign banking institutions, 85 RCBs, 223 RcoBs, 2646 RCCs, 1 postal savings bank, 349 VTBs, 9 lending companies, 37 rural mutual credit cooperatives, 4 financial asset management companies, 63 trust companies, 107 finance companies of corporate groups, 17 financial leasing companies, 4 money brokerage firms and 13 auto financing companies in China (Deng 2011: 3-4). All of them are under the supervision of the CBRC. They are managed by 6 key operational departments, which are listed in the following table; they constitute the main organizational body of the CBRC.

Table 3-1: CBRC's main functional departments

Department	Responsibility
Banking Supervision Department I	Oversee big commercial banks
Banking Supervision Department II	Oversee JSCBs, city commercial banks and city credit unions
Banking Supervision Department III	Oversee foreign banks
Banking Supervision Department IV	Oversee policy banks, China Development Bank, postal savings institutions and asset management companies
Cooperative Finance Supervision Department	Oversee RCCs, rural commercial banks and other new established rural financial institutions
Non-bank Financial Institutions Supervision Department	Oversee trust and investment corporations and other non-bank financial institutions

Source: ICFR 2010: 13

Tasks of the CBRC are summarized here. The CBRC is obligated to formulate supervisory regulations and rules about the establishment, changes, termination and business scope of banking institutions, to license financial institutions, to conduct on-site examination and off-site surveillance of all financial institutions, to conduct fit-and-proper tests of the senior managerial personnel of the banking institutions, to provide proposals on the resolutions of problem deposit-taking institutions and to manage the supervisory boards of the major large commercial banks (ICFR 2010: 12). Furthermore, the CBRC is empowered to take actions against those institutions that fail to comply with prudential supervisory rules by issuing business suspensions, restricting dividend or other payments to shareholders, restricting asset transfers, restricting the power of shareholders, replacing directors or senior managers, withholding approval of branching, in severe cases even taking over the banking institution, facilitating a restructure or closing the banking institution (CBRC 2003d). The enforcement of supervisory regulations has been improved through the delegation of disciplinary authority by the CBRC.

The legal foundation of the supervisory work of the CBRC is the "Law of the People's Republic of China on banking supervision and administration" issued in December 2003 by the CBRC, which is also the first of its kind in China. It officially gave the supervisory authorities the statutory position and standardized supervisory measures and procedures in China (CBRC 2007b: 59). The CBRC should conduct their work within the legal framework defined by the law. The goals of the CBRC are stated in the Law: making sure financial institutions uphold the law, and ensuring the stability of their operations, fair competition among institutions and the trust of the public in such institutions (Cousin 2011: 22). The main source of the law is the "Core principles for effective banking supervision" (the Basel Core Principles) of the Basel Committee of Banking Supervision. The Annual Report of the CBRC stated that half of the main 41 articles embody the concepts of the "Basel Core Principles", in order for the supervision work in China to be in compliance with international standards.

Box 3-1 : **"Core principles for effective banking supervision" of the Basel Committee**

The "Core principles for effective banking supervision" were first published by the Basel Committee in 1997, which represents a systematic summary of best practices of banking supervision in developed counties (CBRC 2007b: 93). In October 2006, the Basel Committee modified and published the revised "Core Principles". There are two purposes of issuance of "Core Principles": one is to provide a set of standards for the International Monetary Fund and the World Bank to review the effectiveness of a country's banking supervision regime; the other is to provide benchmarks by which regulators may judge their own supervisory efforts. The "Basel Core Principles" include 25 most important issues to be taken into consideration when conducting supervisory work and give the guidance for the implementation of supervisory work. Issues mentioned are like rights and status of a supervisory authority, methods to supervise capital adequacy, credit risk, problem assets, country and transfer risk, market risk, liquidity risk etc., supervisory techniques, supervisory reporting and so on. In comparison with the old "Core Principles", the new ones have added principles of comprehensive risk management, management of liquidity risk, interest risk and operational risk. Standards of transparency, governance structure and accountability of supervisors have also been included in the "New Core Principles".

The principles have been accepted by various nations as the guidelines for their establishment and improvement of local banking supervision systems. Most nations conduct a self-assessment of their banking supervision system in light of the "Basel Core Principles" to identify the existing gap in regulatory practice and improve the effectiveness of banking supervision. The CBRC conducts self-assessment every two years regarding the implementation of the "Core Principles for Effective Banking Supervision" (hereinafter the "Core Principles"). Until now the CBRC has conducted five times the self-assessment.

Source: CBRC 2007b: 93/CBRC 2008b: 58

In comparing the supervisory work of the CBRC with that of the PBC, we find that they differ from each other importantly in several respects. First of all, from the regulations published by the CBRC, we can see that the supervision system and the framework in China are designed strictly in line with the requirements of the Basel Accord[1], not as previously under the PBC with the administrative structure (Cai 1999: 169). The aim of the change is to bridge the gap between Chinese and international banking practices. The focus of the supervisory work has also been reset to risk-evaluation. Asset quality, risk managements and technical matters are important points to be checked. The CBRC also use its counter-cyclical policies (such as higher capital buffers and provisioning) to avert financial crisis (Cousin 2011: 25).

It has to be mentioned at last that the CBRC is monitored and supervised by the audit institution and supervisory institutions under the State Council (CBRC 2003d). In this way, the regulation-compliant work of the CBRC is guaranteed by the oversight of the responsible institutions.

3.2 Prudential legal framework of Chinese banking regulation and supervision

A well-developed prudential regulatory framework is the corner stone of effective banking supervision. The Chinese banking legal system consists of laws, administrative regulations, department rules and regulatory rules and guidelines (CBRC 2007b).

The basis of Chinese supervisory framework was set up in 1995. This year is known as the year of financial lawmaking (Deng 2009: 26). Two important laws, namely the "Law of the People's Republic of China on the People's Bank of China" and the "Law of the People's Republic of China on commercial banks", were issued. They would later become the core of China's supervisory system and remained so for a long time. During this period, the State Council and the PBC published a lot of regulations concerning the supervision of the banking sector. These regulations sometimes overlapped with each other and resulted in internal dissonance.
With the establishment of the CBRC, the supervisory framework was radically enlarged and enriched. In December 2003, the first law about the

---

1   That is Basel Accord I more specifically. The Basel Committee of Banking Supervision enacted in 1988 a regulation requiring a minimum capital level of 8% of risk-weighted assets for internationally active banks of G10 countries. The different weights were supposed to reflect the credit risk of the corresponding assets (Rochet 2008: 28).

supervisory work of the CBRC, namely the "Law of the People's Republic of China on banking regulation and supervision", was published. Formally implemented was the law on February 1, 2004. It was the first of its kind in China to systematically standardize the law on the supervision of the banking industry and to lay the foundation for its regulatory system (CBRC 2007b: 59). In 2006, the "Law of the People's Republic of China on banking regulation and supervision" was amended to meet the needs arising from the rapid development of the banking sector.

The aforementioned three laws together make up the legal framework of Chinese banking regulation and supervision. This can be proven through the fact that in most guidance documents and regulations about commercial banks, the first articles will usually note that the regulation is "pursuant to the 'Law of the People's Republic of China on banking regulation and supervision' and the 'Law of the People's Republic of China on commercial banks'". So these laws lay out the foundation for the further development of regulatory framework of the Chinese banking sector.

Table 3-2:   Fundamental laws and regulations about banking institutions

1995 Revised in 2003	"Law of the People's Republic of China on the People's Bank of China"
1995 Revised in 2003	"Law of the People's Republic of China on commercial banks"
2001	"Regulations of the People's Republic of China on foreign financial institutions"
2003 Revised in 2006	"Law of the People's Republic of China on banking regulation and supervision"

Along with these three laws, there is a jungle of regulations, guidelines, rules and notices in this field that is difficult to summarize and clearly outline. The authority itself has never given a clear summary and categorization of its supervisory methods to the public. The regulatory framework is made up of every regulation published by the CBRC since 2003. The "Law of the People's Republic of China on banking regulation and supervision" has only regulated the right and responsibilities of the CBRC and standardized banking supervisory processes and procedures. The regulations of the CBRC dealing with the management of risky issues of financial institutions can better illustrate the supervisory framework in China. In the following chapter, I will summarize the supervisory framework from the perspective of risk management and supervision.

Let us first turn our attention to the most representative risk-related supervisory and regulatory documents. In terms of the oversight of the supervision of risky items, the following regulations were published.

Table 3-3: **Risk-related supervisory and regulatory documents**

2004	"Regulation governing capital adequacy of commercial banks"
2004	"Rules on monitoring and assessment of non-performing assets of commercial banks"
2005	"Guidelines on market risk management of commercial banks"
2006	"Regulations on information system risk management of commercial banks"
2006	"Regulation on compliance risk management of commercial banks"
2007	"Guidelines on operational risk management of commercial banks"
2007	"Guidance on risk-based loan classification"
2009	"Guidelines on liquidity risk management of commercial banks"
2011	"Guidelines on corporate governance of commercial banks (consultative document)"
2011	"Rules governing liquidity risk of commercial banks (tentative)"
2012	"Rules on Capital Management of Commercial Banks (tentative)"

The detailed regulations have covered almost every risky area from credit and market to liquidity and management risks. In these documents, it is regulated in detail what financial institutions should do to mitigate these risks and how supervisory authorities should oversee the implementation of the regulations, which means these regulations contain normally two parts, the management part and the supervision part.

The regulations mentioned above are concerned with specific risk management methods to individual risk items. To check the implementation of the regulations, individual and overall risk assessment programs were developed by the CBRC like "Provisional risk assessment system for JSCBs" in 2004 (see Annex 1). For rural financial institutions, the "Provisional risk assessment and risk forewarning index system for rural cooperative financial institutions" was designed in 2004. In 2005, a document "Core indicators for risk-based supervision of commercial banks (tentative)" pertaining to core indicators of risk supervision of commercial banks was published (see Annex 2). This document clearly defined which indicators are core indicators and has given the minimum requirements for them. These indicators are the benchmarks for carrying out the risk management of commercial banks and a reference system for evaluating, inspecting and forecasting the risks of commercial banks (CBRC 2005d). These indicators were categorized into risk level indicators, risk migration indicators and risk offset indicators instead of risk types as in the former documents. These standards for supervision have been improved in 2011 by the publication of the "New regulatory standards in China's banking industry". A set of new indicators were introduced in this newest document complying with standards used on the international stage. These documents taken together make up an indicator assessment system for the supervision work of the Chinese banking sector. In the following part, I will use these documents as my main reference for the further illustration of the main risk supervision methods used in China.

Table 3-4: **Risk assessment methods and documents issued by the CBRC**

2004	"Provisional risk assessment system for JSCBs"
2004	"Provisional risk assessment and risk forewarning index system for rural cooperative financial institutions"
2005	"Core indicators for risk-based supervision of commercial banks (tentative)"
2011	"New regulatory standards in China's banking industry"

3.3   Prudential supervisory tools of the CBRC

After introducing the legal framework of the prudential supervision, now the exact supervisory indicators and their standards applied by the CBRC will be described. These prudential supervisory indicators are categorized according to supervisory objectives like capital adequacy, credit risk, liquidity risk, corporate governance, profit risk and so on. Most of these indicators are used internationally to evaluate performance and riskiness of a banking institution. Here I will give the definition of these items and their standards set by the CBRC, because there are differences between the internationally used items and the items defined by the CBRC.

3.3.1 Supervision on capital

Capital regulation is now one of the core elements in which all banking supervisory authorities exercise prudential regulation and supervision. The reason for this is because the leverage level of capital of financial institutions is much higher than other industries. In comparison with the assets volume of a financial institution, the capital sum is too limited to cover possible risks. For China, since there is no deposit insurance, adequate capital is the last line of defense against possible losses of a banking institution. From the definition of the CAR and its measurement introduced in China we can see that, the proportion of capital set aside is basically determined by the riskiness of the credit asset.

The PBC adopted the capital adequacy ratio (CAR) measurement method for commercial banks for the first time in 1995. The "Law of the People's Republic of China on commercial banks" (1995) stipulated only the requirement of CAR for commercial banks of more than 8%. This CAR requirement was then rearticulated in the amended "Law of the People's Republic of China on commercial banks" in 2003. Although the PBC had published the minimum CAR requirement in these two documents, the PBC did not give any detailed calculation methods or definitions of its components to the public nor did it enforce adherence (Cousin 2011: 183).

In February 2004, the CBRC officially issued a special regulation relating CAR, namely the "Regulation governing capital adequacy of commercial banks"; the regulation was implemented since March 1, 2004. The capital regulatory framework is hereby diagrammed and decreed. In this regulation, the CAR measurement method and minimum CAR requirement are based on Basel I ("Capital Accord 1998"); Supervisory review, market discipline and information disclosure are designed according to Pillar 2 and Pillar 3 of the Basel II (CBRC 2007b: 69). The publication of this regulation is seen as fundamental and revolutionary in the history of Chinese capital regulation (Cousin 2011: 183). In the following text, I will outline the main elements of the regulation.

In the regulation, the capital adequacy ratio is defined as the ratio of capital held by commercial banks to their risk-weighted assets (CBRC 2004c). Capital, according to the regulation, is divided into core and supplementary capital. To ensure the quality of capital, supplementary capital should not exceed 100% of core capital; long-term subordinated debt in supplementary capital should not exceed 50% of core capital (CBRC 2004c).

Table 3-5:   **Definition of core capital and supplementary capital**

Capital categories	Definition
Core capital	Core capital includes paid-up capital/common stocks, reserves, capital surplus, retained earnings and minority interests.
Supplementary capital	Supplementary capital refers to revaluation reserves, general loan-loss reserves, preference shares, convertible bonds and long-term subordinated debts.

Source: CBRC 2004c

Core CAR and CAR are two indicators used to measure the capital adequacy of commercial banks. They should be no less than 4% and 8% respectively (CBRC 2004c). Calculation formulae of CAR and core CAR are enumerated below--the formulae here are the same as those in the Basel I.

$$CAR = \frac{\text{total capital} - \text{deductions}}{\text{risk-weighted assets} + 12.5 \times \text{capital charge for market risk}}$$

$$\text{Core CAR} = \frac{\text{core capital} - \text{deductions}}{\text{risk-weighted assets} + 12.5 \times \text{capital charge for market risk}}$$

Items like goodwill, equity investments in the unconsolidated financial institutions, on commercial real estate, and in business enterprises shall be deducted from the total capital base when calculating the CAR (CBRC 2004c). Accordingly goodwill, 50% of equity investments in the unconsolidated financial institutions, on commercial real estate and in business enterprises shall be deducted from the core capital base when calculating the core CAR (CBRC 2004c).

In the calculation of CAR ratio, risk weights play an important role in determining the final result. Risk weights here refer to the risk coefficient by which the amount of assets will be multiplied. The risker this asset is, the higher the coefficient will be. Risk weights of different assets are regulated in the second annex of this regulation. "They were set similar to those promoted under Basel I for on-balance and off-balance sheet exposures." (Cousin 2011: 185) A big step taken by the regulators is the removal of the preferential treatment of SOEs, which now receive the same risk weight as other enterprises (Cousin 2011: 185). Table 3-6 shows the risk weights of the on-balance credit items. Besides them, capital should also be set aside for credit risks of off-balance items in the way of converting each off-balance sheet item to credit equivalents by multiplying the nominal principal amounts by a credit conversion factor (CBRC 2004c). Market risk is also taken into account for banks with trading positions exceeding 10% of the bank's on- and off-balance sheet assets or RMB 8.5 billion (CBRC 2004c).

Table 3-6:   **Risk weights of on-balance sheet assets**

Items	Risk weight
a. Cash	
Cash in vault	0%
gold	0%
Deposits at the PBC	0%
b. Claims on central government and central bank	
Claims on the Chinese government	0%
Claims on the PBC	0%
Claims on the foreign central government and foreign central banks, where the rating for the sovereign or region is AA- or higher	0%
Claims on the foreign central governments and foreign central banks, where the rating for the sovereign or region is below AA-	100%
c. Claims on public-sector entities (not including commercial companies)	
Claims on public-sector entities invested by central governments and central banks, where the rating for the sovereign or region is AA- or higher	50%
Claims on pubic-sector entities invested by central governments and central banks, where the rating for the sovereign or region is below AA-	100%
Claims on domestic public-sector entities invested by the Chinese central government	50%
Claims on other public-sector entities	100%
d. Claims on domestically incorporated financial institutions	
Claims on domestically incorporated policy banks	0%
Claims on Asset management companies (AMC) invested by the Chinese central government	0%
Claims on specific debs issued by the AMCs to purchase the state owned banks' non-performance loans	0%

74

Items	Risk weight
Other claims on AMCs invested by the Chinese central government	100%
Claims on domestically incorporated commercial banks with an original maturity of four months or shorter	0%
Claims on domestically incorporated commercial banks with an original maturity over four months	20%
e. Claims on financial institutions incorporated in other countries or regions	
Claims on commercial banks/securities firms, where the rating for the sovereign or region is AA- or higher	20%
Claims on commercial banks/securities firms, where the rating for the sovereign or region is below AA-	100%
Claims on multilateral development banks	0%
Claims on other financial institutions	100%
f. Claims on business enterprises and individuals	
Claims on residential mortgage	50%
Claims on other business enterprises and individuals	100%
g. Claims on others	100%

Source: CBRC 2004c

According to the CAR level, banks are categorized into three classes as shown in Table 3-7. These minimum capital requirements of 8% should be met by commercial banks by January 1, 2007 according to the regulation (CBRC 2004c).

Table 3-7:   **Categories of banks according to their CAR and core CAR in the regulation published in 2004**

Categories	Minimum capital requirement
Adequately capitalized banks	The CAR is not less than 8%, And the core CAR is not less than 4%.
Undercapitalized banks	The CAR is less than 8%, Or the core CAR is less than 4%.
Significantly undercapitalized banks	The CAR is less than 4%, Or the core CAR is less than 2%.

Source: CBRC 2004c

In the latest published "Guiding opinions on the implementation of new regulatory standards in China's banking industry" of 2011 and the "Rules on capital management of commercial banks" – the first order of the CBRC in 2012 – the standards for CAR were reset to be in compliance with the Basel III.

The "Rules on capital management of commercial banks" (hereinafter "Rules") can be seen as an improved version of the earlier "Regulation governing capital adequacy of commercial banks" published in 2004. These new rules will be implemented from January 1, 2013. In the "Rules", the calculation method was updated according to the Basel II and Basel III:

CAR

$$= \frac{\text{total capital} - \text{deductions}}{\begin{array}{c}\text{risk-weighted assets} \\ +12.5 \times \text{capital charge for market risk} \\ +12.5 \times \text{capital charge for operational risk}\end{array}} \times 100\%$$

Tier-1 CAR

$$= \frac{\text{tier-1 capital} - \text{deductions}}{\begin{array}{c}\text{risk-weighted assets} \\ +12.5 \times \text{capital charge for market risk} \\ +12.5 \times \text{capital charge for operational risk}\end{array}} \times 100\%$$

Core tier-1 CAR

$$= \frac{\text{core tier-1 capital} - \text{deductions}}{\begin{array}{c}\text{risk-weighted assets} \\ +12.5 \times \text{capital charge for market risk} \\ +12.5 \times \text{capital charge for operational risk}\end{array}} \times 100\%$$

In comparison with the formulae used since 2004, operational risk was also integrated into risky assets. Furthermore, capital is divided into core tier-1 capital, other tier-1 capital and tier-2 capital. The minimum CAR for core tier-1 capital, tier-1 capital and capital were set up at 5%, 6% and 8% respectively (CBRC 2011a). On the base of minimum capital ratio, commercial banks are required to reserve 2.5% capital conservation buffer besides 0-2.5% as a countercyclical capital buffer upon the minimum capital requirement to encounter possible fluctuations and risks in the market (CBRC 2011b). Both the 2.5% capital conservation buffer and the 0-2.5% countercyclical capital buffer should be core-1 capital.

When the capital conservation buffer is added to the CAR minimum ratio of 8%, CAR of banks should reach 10.5% at a minimum to satisfy the requirement. Systematically important banks (SIBs) should reserve 1% more tier-1 capital than non-SIBs (CBRC 2011b). So the CAR of SIBs should not be lower than 11.5% and the CAR for non-SIBs should not be lower than 10.5%. In this case, the $0 - 2.5\%$ countercyclical capital buffer is not taken into consideration. Banks were required to implement new capital regulatory standards from the beginning of 2012. SIBs and non-SIBs should meet the requirements by the end of 2013 and the end of 2016 respectively. The change of CAR requirements is summarized in Table 3-8.

Table 3-8: **Changes of minimum CAR standards for commercial banks**

Year and regulation/CAR items	Minimum core tier-1 CAR	Minimum tier-1 CAR	Minimum core CAR	Minimum CAR
1995-2004 in the "Law of the People's Republic of China on commercial banks"				8%
2004 in the "Regulation governing capital adequacy of commercial banks"			4%	8%
2011 in the "New regulatory standards in China's banking industry" and 2012 in the "Rules on capital management of commercial banks"	5%	6%		8% SIBs: 11.5% Non-SIBs:10.5%

Source: CBRC 2004c/CBRC: 2011a

New standards for CAR of commercial banks were set up with the publication of the two documents mentioned above. The new domestic regulatory standards and structure arrangements regarding CAR are largely consistent with Basel III, except for two differences (CBRC 2011b). First, the domestic minimum requirement on core tier-1 CAR is 0.5% higher than that prescribed in Basel III. Second, the CAR of SIBs is 1% higher than that of non-SIBs, while the Basel Committee and Financial Stability Board (FSB) have not yet reached a consensus in this regard (CBRC 2011b). Basel III requires its members to start the implementation of new capital regulatory standards as of the beginning of 2013 and fully meet the standards by the end of 2018, while the Guiding Opinions (2012) require the banks to start the implementation as of the beginning of 2012 and meet the standards by the end of 2016 (CBRC 2011b). The Guiding Opinions (2012) require implementation 1 year ahead of schedule and compliance 2 years ahead of schedule (CBRC 2011b).

We then can consider the real situation of the CAR level of Chinese financial institutions. Table 3-9 shows the CAR levels categorized according to the types of financial institutions. From 2003 to 2009, foreign banks were better capitalized than native Chinese banks; SOCBs occupy a better position than JSCBs. Since only RCCs with good performance were allowed to transfer into rural commercial banks during the RCC reform, they are better capitalized from inception than RCCs. RcoBs, likewise, surpass RCCs' capitalization. The newly established PSBC, totally owned by the China Post Group, has the least CAR. Foreign banks, on the other side, acquired the best score in CAR, and their CARs have also reached international standards. Although China has introduced the CAR as a supervisory target, only commercial banks are required to meet the minimum requirements by January 1, 2007.

Table 3-9: **CAR of all Chinese banks from 2003 to 2009**

Unit: %

Banks/Jahr	2003	2004	2005	2006	2007	2008	2009
SOCBs	4.06	4.25	4.58	5.59	5.62	6.15	5.45
JSCBs	3.30	3.13	2.99	3.50	4.67	5.00	4.78
City commercial banks	3.41	3.42	4.06	4.69	5.64	6.46	6.32
RCBs	1.22	4.78	5.14	4.94	5.41	5.75	5.98
RcoBs			6.42	6.34	6.35	6.51	6.65
Urban credit cooperatives (UCCs)	0.27	1.14	1.55	2.74	4.89	5.84	6.36
RCCs	-0.52	2.38	4.20	4.34	4.30	4.26	4.27
PSBC					0.68	1.00	1.23
Foreign banks	9.82	8.48	8.73	8.05	9.36	10.56	12.41
Chinese banks combined	**3.25**	**3.66**	**4.10**	**4.87**	**5.16**	**5.59**	**5.19**

Source: Cousin 2011: 182

Since the regulation is directed towards commercial banks only, Table 3-10 isolates the situation of commercial banks in China. The CAR data gathered from the annual reports of the CBRC and a report delivered by the assistant director-general of Banking Supervision Department III of the CBRC in the "Multi-year Expert Meeting on Services, Development and Trade" held by the United Nations will show us, how the capital adequacy situation in China banking industry really is. From 2003 to 2011, the average CAR level of all Chinese commercial banks increased steadily. Within only 5 years from 2003, the average level of CAR was raised from -3.0% to 8.3%. In 2003, there were only 8 which had fulfilled the 8% CAR requirement, while since 2009 100% of commercial banks have achieved the standards. Furthermore, in 2010 and 2011, the average CAR of all commercial banks in China even exceeded the 11.5% minimum CAR level for SIBs.

Table 3-10: **Average CAR of Chinese commercial banks from 2003 to 2011**

Year	Average CAR	Number of banks meeting the CAR requirement	Proportion of banks meeting the CAR requirement
2003	-3.0%	8	0.6%
2004	0.0%	30	47.5%
2005	4.9%	53	75.1%
2006	7.3%	100	77.4%
2007	8.3%	161	79.0%
2008	12.0%	204	99.9%
2009	11.4%	239	100%
2010	12.2%	281	100%
2011	12.7%	390	100%

Source: Deng 2011/CBRC 2011e: 27/2012a: 25

At the beginning, the state contributed substantially to the quick increase of CAR. The Financial Ministry of China issued RMB 279 billion special national debts to SOCBs to replenish their capital in 1998 (Zhou / Kang 2011). Later, with the commercialization of Chinese banking industry, commercial banks acquired the necessary capital either by looking for new shareholders (e.g. through initial publishing offerings), pressing the present ones for new capital or issuing long-term subordinated debts and hybrid bonds (Cousin 2011: 186). In the notice issued by the CBRC in 2009, the ratio of long-term subordinated bonds to the core capital was capped at 25% (CBRC 2009c). Banks with a CAR below 7% and non-nationwide banks with a CAR below 5% would not be allowed to make use of subordinated debts to replenish capital (CBRC 2009c). The structure of capital in Chinese banks is characterized by big share of core capital in the whole capital amount, high proportion of common stocks and low levels of retained earnings in the amount of core capital. Table 3-11 demonstrates that average core capital of commercial banks accounted for almost four times the supplementary capital in 2010 and 2011, while the international big banks had on average 60% common stock and 25% subordinated loans in their capital (Zhou / Kang 2011). Former deputy governor of the PBC Xiaoling Wu assigned the poor development of the Chinese capital market as the reason for the high proportion of core capital (Wu 2010). "Because of the poor development of capital market, there are no enough subordinated debts served as resources for the capital funding", said Wu (Wu 2010).

Table 3-11: **Capital information of all commercial banks in 2010 and 2011**

Unit: RMB billion and %

Items/Year	2010	2011
Core capital	4298.51	5336.66
Supplementary capital	129.45	1441.76
Capital deductions	319.64	373.54
On-balance sheet risk-weighted assets	35537.11	43142.07
Off-balance sheet risk-weighted assets	5323.37	6881.90
Market risk capital	27.33	29.63
CAR	**12.2**	**12.7**
Core CAR	**10.1**	**10.2**

Source: CBRC 2012a: 128

Overall, the supervisory instrument CAR forces financial institutions to improve their asset quality instead of increasing the asset amount. If they do not want to face excessive funding pressure, they must reduce the proportion of risky assets and make their credit structure safer. Sacrificed are their profits to ensure safety in the whole system. The implementation of the CAR minimum requirement costs much for banks, but a risk-sensitive approach to business is contained in it and this will help banks draw a competitive advantage and smoother entry in other foreign markets. According to the information disclosure requirement, the CBRC will get more information and data for a more accurate overview and understanding of banks' risks and potential losses (Cousin 2011: 188). The Basel II is unlikely to protect the finance industry from system-wide collapse or to reduce the amount of money, authorities would need to spend, if a bailout is again deemed necessary (Cousin 2011: 188).

3.3.2 Supervision on liquidity risk

The liquidity risk is a birthmark of banks that arises from funding of long-term assets by short-term liabilities. The definition of liquidity risk given by the Basel Committee in the "Principles of sound liquidity risk" issued in September 2009 is "the ability of a bank to fund increase in assets and meet obligations as they come due, without incurring unacceptable losses" (Oracle 2009). The ways to manage liquidity of financial institutions include assets management, liabilities management and integrated management of both assets and liabilities. The aim of liquidity management is on the one hand to ensure that enough liquidity is available to meet due obligations from depositors and to satisfy financial needs from qualified debtors, and on the other to ensure that the least possible assets are kept in liquid form since liquid assets are characterized by low profitability and high tradability in the inter-bank market like assets in the form of cash, public debts or deposits in other banks.

China has published two documents to illustrate how to manage liquidity in commercial banks. In 2009, the "Guidelines on liquidity risk management of commercial banks" were issued and then in 2011 the "Guidelines" were updated to the "Rules governing liquidity risk management of commercial banks (tentative)", both published by the CBRC. These two documents constitute the legal framework of Chinese liquidity management and supervision. In the liquidity management part of the "Rules", the board of directors and the senior management team in a financial institution are regulated as the main responsible organs for liquidity management. Their responsibilities are clearly defined. Important management measures of liquidity are descripted. The biggest change in the "Rules" in comparison with the "Guidelines" is that the supervisory part in the "Rules" has been expanded to define the main supervisory indicators, set up limits for these indicators and provide a detailed description of supervision methods and procedures of the CBRC. Furthermore, new liquidity indicators have been introduced, namely liquidity coverage ratio (LCR) and net stable funding ratio (NSFR) into off-site surveillance in China benchmarking against the latest supervisory standards issued by the BCBS in the international framework for liquidity risk measurement, standards and monitoring in Basel III. "These measures should assess the likely standing of the banks under stress." (Cousin 2011: 191) As one of the G20 countries, China is obligated to follow the requirement of Basel III. Moreover, structures of assets and liabilities of domestic banks in China are increasingly diversified as existing indicators on liquidity risk are no longer sufficient to identify liquidity risks (CBRC 2011b). Thereby the country has also introduced the two indicators in the newest edition of the liquidity risk supervisory document. The minimum requirements for these two indicators are 100%. Commercial banks should meet the supervisory standards of liquidity risk management before the end of 2013 and adopt the NSFR no later than the end of 2016 (CBRC 2011d). The "Rules" have been effect since January 1, 2012.

In the following test, I will briefly introduce the calculation methods of the main indicators and the requirements of these indicators, which are mentioned not only in the "Rules governing liquidity risk management of commercial banks", but also in the "Guiding opinions on the implementation of new regulatory standards in China's banking industry" issued in 2011, the "Core indicators for risk-based supervision of commercial canks" from 2006 and "Provisional risk assessment system for JSCBs" from 2004. These four documents are the main references for the description of the following indicators.

Table 3-12:   Main liquidity risk indicators and their limits set by the CBRC

Liquidity risk indicators	Calculation formulae and their limit set by the CBRC
Loan-to-deposit ratio	$$\text{Loan-to-deposit ratio} = \frac{\text{loans}}{\text{depostis}} \leq 75\%$$ Loan-to-deposit ratio refers to the proportion between loans and deposits of a financial institution. It's a common parameter used to evaluate the ability of a bank to cover withdrawals made by its consumers and control available liquid assets of a financial institution. In China, this ratio should be no higher than 75%.
Liquidity ratio	$$\text{Liduidity ratio} = \frac{\text{liquid assets}}{\text{liquid liabilities}} \geq 25\%$$ The liquidity ratio refers to the proportion between the balance of liquid assets and balance of liquid liabilities which shall be 25% or higher. The higher the liquidity ratio is recorded, the more liquid a bank is. The overall level of commercial banks' liquidity is assessed by it. Liquid assets consist of cash, gold, excess deposit reserves, net assets after inter-bank transaction differences to be mature within one month, receivable interests and other receivables to be mature within one month, pass loans to be mature within one month, securities investments to be mature within one month, bond investments convertible at any time at the secondary market domestic or abroad, as well as other convertible assets to be mature within one month (excluding non-performing assets). Liquid liabilities consist of the current deposits, time deposits to be mature within one month, net liabilities after inter-bank transaction differences to be mature within one month, issued bonds to be mature within one month, payable interests and all the accounts payable to be mature within one month, loans from the Central Bank to be mature within one month, as well as other liabilities to be mature within one month.

Continuation

Table3-12: **Main liquidity risk indicators and their limits set by the CBRC**

Liquidity gap ratio	Liquidity gap ratio $$= \frac{\text{liquidity gap}}{\text{on-balance-sheet and off-balance-sheet assets to be mature within 90 days}}$$ $$\geq -10\%$$ The liquidity gap = the balance of non-balance-sheet and off-balance-sheet assets to be mature within 90 days – the on-balance-sheet and off-balance-sheet liabilities to be mature within 90 days. This indicator shows the liquidity surplus or shortfall for each observed projection period, e.g. each individual day or on individual reference dates. The liquidity gap ratio should be -10% or higher, which means that the shortfall of assets in proportion with the total assets should not be less than 10%. The comparison is performed in a normal scenario. In addition to a normal scenario, most banks forecast a liquidity gap under certain stress conditions (Deutsche Bundesbank: 12).
Core liability dependency	Core liability dependency $$= \frac{\text{core liabilities}}{\text{total liabilities}}$$ $$\geq 60\%$$ Core liability dependency ratio refers to the proportion between core liabilities and total liabilities which shall be 60% or higher. The so-called core liabilities include time deposits with remaining maturities within three months or longer, the issued bonds, and 50% of demand deposits. The term "total liabilities" means the balance of all liabilities in the balance sheet constituted in accordance with the accounting system for financial enterprises.

Continuation
Table 3-12: **Main liquidity risk indicators and their limits set by the CBRC**

Liquidity coverage ratio	$$LCR = \frac{\text{stock of high-quality liquid assets}}{\text{total net cash outflows over the next 30 calendar days}}$$ $$\geq 100\%$$ The liquidity coverage ratio (LCR) refers to the ratio of the stock of high-quality liquid assets to the total net cash outflows over the next 30 calendar days. This standard aims to ensure that a bank maintains an adequate level of unencumbered, high-quality liquid assets that can be converted into cash to meet its liquidity needs for a 30 calendar day time horizon under a significantly severe liquidity stress scenario specified by supervisors(BCBS 2010: 3). The standard requires that the value of the ratio should not be lower than 100%. The CBRC also set the same requirement to the banking sector in China. Assets are considered to be high-quality liquid assets if they can be easily and immediately converted into cash at little or no loss of value.
Net Stable Funding Ratio	$$NSFR = \frac{\text{available amount of stable funding}}{\text{required amount of stable funding}}$$ $$\geq 100\%$$ The NSFR is defined as the amount of available amount of stable funding to the amount of required stable funding. This ratio must be greater than 100% according to the Basel requirement. Here stable funding is defined as the portion of those types and amounts of equity and liability financing expected to be reliable sources of funds over a one-year time horizon under conditions of extended stress(BCBS 2010: 25). The required amount of such funding required is a function of the liquidity characteristics of various types of assets held, off-balance sheet contingent exposures incurred and/or the activities pursued by the institution. The objective of the introduction of NSFR is to promote more medium and long-term funding of the assets and activities of banking organizations. This metric establishes a minimum acceptable amount of stable funding based on the liquidity characteristics of an institution's assets and activities over a one year horizon.

Source: CBRC 2011d /BCBS 2010: 3 & 25/CBRC 2005d

Among these indicators, the deposit-to-loan ratio is an old liquidity indicator used by the Chinese supervisory authorities. The ratio as a basic liquidity indicator guarantees that banks will not overly extend loans without considering the possible liquidity risk. In the "Law of the People's Republic of China on commercial banks" published in 1995, the deposit-to-loan ratio was set to never exceed 75% for commercial banks. For RCCs, the ABC published the "Interim rules governing credit funds of RCCs" in 1987. RCCs were also required to keep the ratio of loans to the sum of deposits and its own capital under 75% from 1987. The following table shows that the loan-to-deposit ratio of banking institutions in China has complied with the 75% obligation since 2004. Only in 2003, the ratio has exceeded the limit. RCCs on the other hand have maintained their loan-to-deposit ratio from 1998 to 2004 between 68% and 72% (Zhao 2008: 124).

Figure 3-3: **Loan-to-deposit ratio of Chinese banking industry from 2003 to 2011**

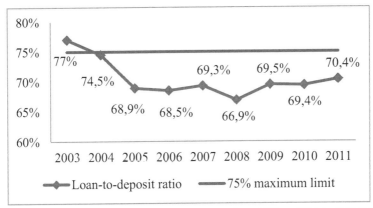

Source: calculated according to deposits and loans from 2003 to 2011 in CBRC 2012a: 122

Indicators check the availability of liquid assets from different perspectives. The loan-to-deposit ratio is an indirect ratio of liquidity, while liquidity gap ratio, liquidity ratio and liquidity coverage ratio directly measure the liquid level of assets on different time horizons. The liquidity ratio checks the proportion of liquid assets against the liquid liabilities. The liquidity gap ratio checks whether there are enough assets to cover possible due liabilities in an interval of 90 days. The two indicators overlap with each other and their essential difference is only in the definition of liquid assets and liquid liabilities. The Liquidity coverage ratio (LCR) is newly introduced in the Chinese banking industry. The LCR is differentiated from the liquidity ratio in the way that the LCR calculates high-quality assets as liquid assets and only net cash outflow is counted as dividend. Furthermore, the paradigm is also different from the liquidity ratio in the way that the LCR is calculated under severe liquidity stress scenario specified by supervisors. In comparison with liquidity ratio, the LCR is a more precise and fine-tuned indicator, and definitions of both assets and liabilities are narrower. The aim of the LCR is to check if enough easily convertible assets are available to cover cash outflows in the following 30 days under a stress situation. The LCR was introduced on January 1, 2012, and all commercial banks should reach the 100% requirement of the LCR by the end of 2013 (CBRC 2011d).

Currently only liquidity ratio data is available in the "Annual report of the CBRC". This indicator has been active in China for a long time as has the loan-to-deposit ratio and was already regulated in the "Law of the People's Republic of China on commercial banks" in 1995 which set the minimum requirement at 25%. The following table illustrates that the average liquidity ratio of Chinese banking institutions has been above the minimum requirement of 25% from 2007 to 2011. The liquidity ratio of Chinese commercial banks is a little bit lower than the liquidity ratio of all banking institutions.

Table 3-13:   **Liquidity ratio of Chinese banking institutions from 2007 to 2012**

Unit: %

Institutions/Year	2007	2008	2009	2010	2011	2012
Banking institutions	40.3	49.8	45.7	43.7	44.7	47.8
Commercial banks	37.7	46.1	42.4	42.2	43.2	45.8

Source: CBRC 2012a: 124/CBRC 2013b: 169

Core liability ratio checks the percentage of relatively long-term and safer liabilities against the whole amount of liabilities of a financial institution. The higher the core liability ratio records, the more stable and secure the liabilities are supposed to be. This ratio is not internationally accepted. This ratio is mentioned in the "Core indicators for risk-based supervision of commercial banks" once, but then disappeared in the regulation field. No results relating this indicator are currently available.

Through the implementation of multi-dimensional liquidity risk supervision indicators, the CBRC aims to establish a system of liquidity risk controls and monitoring indicators that incorporate multiple scenarios, methods, currencies and time-spans (CBRC 2011a). The CBRC also conformed its own liquidity supervisory system to the international standards with the introduction of new indicators. Although only data about loan-to-deposit ratio and liquidity ratio are available, we can conclude from the declining line of loan-to-deposit ratio and high liquidity ratio that most of the banks are adequately liquid. In the annual report of the CBRC, the Chinese supervisory authority even evaluated Chinese commercial banks as over-liquid (CBRC 2008b: 77) in recent years. Bell and Chao commented in their research that the liquidity of Chinese banks is better positioned in comparison with banks in other countries (Bell/Chao 2010).

3.3.3 Supervision on credit risk

Credit risk is the most significant risk threatening the security of the Chinese financial system. The supervision of credit risk is the basic work of banking institutions and the CBRC. Traditional methods to supervise credit risk include monitoring the ratio of NPLs and regulating the highest amount of loans extended to a client. In recent years the regulatory framework for credit risk supervision has enormously expanded and new indicators were introduced to better monitor the situation of credit risk. Table 3-15 shows some of the basic regulations related to credit risk supervision which will be used in this part. The CBRC has also published a set of special administrative and supervisory regulations especially for some kinds of loan types. Because of their irrelevance with this part, these regulations are not listed.

Table 3-14:   Basic regulatory framework of credit risk supervision

Regulations about loan classification	"Accounting rules of financial and insurance companies" (Ministry of Finance 1993)
	"Guidelines on risk-based loan classification" for commercial banks (PBC 2001)
	"Guidelines on risk-based loan classification of rural cooperative financial institutions" (CBRC 2006)
	"Guidelines on risk-based loan classification" (CBRC 2007)
Regulations about loan loss provision	"Guidance on provisioning for loan losses"(PBC 2002)
Regulation about non-performing assets' monitoring	"Provisional rules monitoring and assessment of non-performing assets of commercial banks" (CBRC 2004)
	"Rules on monitoring and assessment of non-performing assets of Rural Credit Cooperatives" (CBRC 2007)
Other related regulations	"Administrative rules governing the connected lending between commercial banks and their insiders/shareholders" (CBRC 2004)

Before introducing the indicators used for the monitoring of credit risks, one important change in the loan classification should be introduced. Loan classification method will decide directly the amount of NPLs, so a stringent loan classification method is of vital importance. Before 2002, loans of commercial banks were classified into pass, overdue, idle and bad loans according to the "Accounting rules of financial and insurance companies" published by the Ministry of Finance in China in 1993. Overdue loans refer to loans, whose principal and interest cannot be paid on time (PBC 1996). Idle loans refer to loans whose principal has not been paid for over two years or whose business or projects supported have already been called off (PBC 1996). Bad loans are loans that have no possibility to be collected again (PBC 1996). Overdue, idle and bad loans belong to the category NPLs. The main criteria used in the old loan classification method are the repayment of principal and interest and whether debtors can keep the terms prescribed in the loan contract. It can be seen as an ex-post loan classification method since the classification could only be made when loans fell due. The old loan classification system has been criticized for its emphasis on loans over borrowers, on principal over interest re-payments and on the occurrence of a default event over the true riskiness of the borrower and transaction (Cousin 2011: 157). The old four-tier loan classification method cannot truly reflect the level of NPLs.

In 1998 the new risk-based loan classification method was first piloted in commercial banks of Guangdong Province. Nationwide application of the new classification system in commercial banks was realized on January 1, 2002. The ABC and rural financial institutions did not engage in the appli-cation of risk-based loan classification system until 2003 and 2006 respec-tively because of their unfavorable loan situation. The PBC officially pub-lished the "Guidelines on risk-based loan classification" to guide the prac-tice in December 2001. The new loan classification method refers to a process of categorizing loans of commercial banks according to their risk (PBC 2001). Different from the old classification system, loans are graded into 5 categories in the new system based on the inherent risks, namely pass, special mention, substandard, doubtful and loss loans. The last three categories belong to NPLs. This classification method is compliant with international acknowledged loan classification standard. The primary fac-tors deciding loan categories include repayment ability of borrowers, cred-it records of borrowers, borrower's willingness to repay, guarantee of loans, legal obligations of loan repayment and credit management of banks (PBC 2001). Table 3-15 sets forth the five classification categories and their corresponding definitions. In 2007, the CBRC updated the PBC's "Guidelines on risk-based loan classification" which is applicable not only for commercial banks but also rural cooperative financial institu-tions, village or township banks, lending companies (CBRC 2007d).

Table 3-15:   Five-tier loan classification system in China

Loan types	Five-tier categories	Definition
Performing loans	Pass	Borrowers can keep the terms of their loans. There is no reason to doubt their ability to repay principal and interest in full and on a timely basis.
	Special mention (SM)	Borrowers currently are still able to service the debt but some factors could impede repayment
Non-performing loans	Substandard	Borrower's ability to service loans is apparently in question. Borrower cannot depend on its normal business revenues to pay back the principal and interest and certain losses might inure even when guarantees are executed.
	Doubtful	Collection of principal and interest in full is improbable, significant losses certain, collateral to be collected
	Loss	Principal and interest of loans cannot be recovered or only a small portion can be recovered after taking all possible measures and resorting to necessary legal procedures.

Source: Cousin 2011: 159/PBC 2001

Loan classification is the precondition for the credit management. Based on the new loan classification regulation of 2001, the PBC further published the "Guidance on provisioning for loan losses" in 2002 and required all banks to set aside adequate provisions for loan losses. According to the "Guidance" loan loss provisions include general, special and specific reserves (PBC 2002). General reserves are funds set aside on quarterly basis to cover unidentified possible loan loss (PBC 2002). As of the end of the year the outstanding general reserves should not be less than 1% of outstanding loans (PBC 2002). Special reserves should set asset to cover special losses sourced from the last four categories of loans according to the new loan classification method. The amount of special reserves should be 2% of special mention loans, 25% of substandard loans, 50% of doubtful loans and 100% of loss loans (PBC 2002). Provisions for losses of substandard or doubtful loans can be set lower or higher than the norm in a range of 20% (PBC 2002). Specific reserves are funds set aside covering losses out of risks of a state, region, an industry or a type of loans (PBC 2002). The amount of specific reserves should be decided by banks in their discretion. As I have mentioned before capital adequacy is the last line of defense against any losses of a banking institution, whereas loan loss provision should be seen as the first line of defense against loan losses. Loan losses should be written off first using the funds of loan loss conserves and then banking institutions' revenues. When there are still loan losses not written off, capital should be put into use.

The information about loan classification and loan loss provision introduced above is the precondition for the credit risk supervision. In the following text main risk supervisory indicators will be introduced. Credit risk indicators can be categorized according to their usage into indicators to measure asset quality, loan concentration level, credit migration and loan loss provision (see Table 3-16). The standards set here are from the latest regulation either from the "Core indicators for risk-based supervision of commercial banks" (2005) or "New regulatory standards in China's banking industry" (2011), so the requirements are very high.

Table 3-16:   Credit risk indicators

Cate-gories	Credit risk indicators	Calculation formulae and their limit set by the CBRC
Indicators to measure asset quality	Ratio of non-performing assets (NPAs)	Ratio of NPAs $$= \frac{\text{non-performing assets}}{\text{total amount of assets}}$$ $$\leq 4\%$$ The ratio of non-performing assets refers to the proportion between non-performing assets and the total amount of assets which shall be not higher than 4% according to the "Core indicators for risk-based supervision of commercial banks" (2005). Non-performing assets consist of non-performing credit assets and non-performing non-credit assets in the balance sheet of a bank. This indicator is a first-class indicator with a subordinated second-class indicator of ratio of NPLs. Data of ratio of non-performing assets is seldom opened to the public.
	Ratio of NPLs	Ratio of NPLs $$= \frac{\text{substandard loans} + \text{doubtful loans} + \text{loss loans}}{\text{total loans}}$$ $$\leq 5\%$$ This indicator is often used to evaluate credit quality of a bank and the credit riskiness of the financial system. According to the "Core indicators for risk-based supervision of commercial banks" (2005), the ratio of NPLs was set to be no higher than 5%.
Indicators to measure concentration risk	Credit concentration ratio of a single group client	Credit concentration ratio of a single group client $$= \frac{\text{total credit amount of the largest group client}}{\text{net capital}}$$ $$\leq 15\%$$ The credit concentration ratio of a single group client refers to the proportion between the total credit amount of the largest group client and the net capital of the bank which shall be 15% or lower according to the "Core indicators for risk-based supervision of commercial banks". This indicator is a first-class indicator with a subordinate second-class indicator the loan concentration ratio of a single client.

	Continuation	
	Loan concentration ratio of a single client	Loan concentration ratio of a single client $$= \frac{\text{total amount of loans of the largest client}}{\text{net capital}}$$ $$\leq 10\%$$ The loan concentration ratio of a single client refers to the proportion between the total loan amount of the largest client and the net capital which shall be 10% or lower according to the "Core indicators for risk-based supervision of commercial banks".
Indicators to measure concentration risk	Overall ratio of connected lending	Overall ratio of connected lending $$= \frac{\text{total amount of credits of all related parties}}{\text{net capital}}$$ $$\leq 50\%$$ This ratio refers to the proportion between the generalized credits granted to related parties of a bank and the net capital which shall be 50% or lower according to the "Core indicators for risk-based supervision of commercial banks" (2005). This ratio is used to check how much credit is granted to the related parties of a bank. It should be controlled within a maximum limit. Related parties here include natural persons, legal persons and other organizations, who are either insiders or shareholders of the bank. Clear definition of related parties can be found in the "Administrative rules governing the connected lending between commercial banks and their insiders/sharcholders" published by the CBRC in 2004. The term "total amount of credits of all relevant parties" means the balance of credits of all the related parties of commercial banks deducted deposit guarantees, bank certificates as collateral and government bonds provided by the related parties when they apply for a credit.

Indicators to measure risk migration	Continuation	
	Migration ratio of pass loans	Migration ratio of pass loans $$= \frac{\text{loan amount migrated to the lower grades}}{\text{balance of pass loans at the}}$$ from the pass laosns in an observation period end of the observation period This is the proportion of pass loans which move from pass loan category to the next categories. Different from the indicators above migration indicators are dynamic indicators which describe the change of loans in different categories. It can better reflect the situation of loans and their changes.
	Migration ratio of special mention loans	Migration ratio of special mention loans $$= \frac{\text{amount migrated to the lower grades from}}{\text{balance of special mention loans at the end}}$$ the special mention loans in an observation period of the observation period This indicator refers to the proportion of special mention loans which move from special mention loan category to the next categories at the end of the observation period.
	Migration ratio of substandard loans	Migration ratio of substandard loans $$= \frac{\text{amount migrated to the lower grades from}}{\text{balance of substandard loans at the end}}$$ the substandard loans in an observation period of the observation period This indicator refers to the proportion of substandard loans which move from substandard loan category to the next loan categories at the end of the observation period.
	Migration ratio of doubtful loans	Migration ratio of doubtful loans $$= \frac{\text{amount migrated to loss loans from the}}{\text{balance of doubtful loans at the end}}$$ doubtful loans in an observation period of the observation period This indicator refers to the proportion of doubtful loans which move from doubtful loan category to loss loan category at the end of the observation period.

Indicators for loan loss provision	Continuation	
	Loan loss provision ratio	loan loss provision ratio $= \dfrac{\text{amount of loan loss provision}}{\text{all loans}}$ $\geq 2.5\%$
	Loan loss provision coverage ratio	Loan loss provision coverage ratio $= \dfrac{\text{general reserves} + \text{specific reserves} + \text{special reserves}}{\text{amount of NPLs}}$ $\geq 150\%$
		Minimum requirements for loan loss provision ratio and loan loss provision coverage ratio were sourced from the "New regulatory standards in China's banking industry" published by the CBRC in 2011. The standards of these two indicators are compliant with the requirements of Basel III. These requirements were put into practice since January 1, 2012. For SIBs these requirements should be met as of end of 2013; for non-SIBs requirements should be met within differentiated transitional period.

Source: CBRC 2006a/CBRC 2011a/CBRC 2005d

Overall speaking, the supervisory framework and their requirements can be compared with international standards. The real implementation situation of these standards can be shown from the following data. By the end of 2012 the total NPLs of all banking institutions in China amounted to RMB 1074.63 billion, which is 1.6% of total outstanding loans (see Table 3-17). From the structure of NPLs we can see that substandard and doubtful loans made up the biggest part of the total NPLs. So from the perspective of NPL ratio and NPL structure, the whole Chinese banking sector shows a very positive loan quality by the end of 2012.

Table 3-17:   **NPLs of all banking institutions from 2010 to 2012**

Unit: RMB billion and %

Item/Year	2010	2011	2012
Outstanding balance of NPLs	1243.70	1053.34	1074.63
Substandard	585.25	478.43	527.06
Doubtful	496.78	440.09	438.67
Loss	161.67	134.81	108.90
NPL ratio	2.4	1.8	1.6
Substandard	1.1	0.8	0.8
Doubtful	1.0	0.7	0.6
Loss	0.3	0.2	0.2

Source: CBRC 2013b: 168

Figure 3-4 shows the development of NPLs of commercial banks from 2005 to 2012. Commercial banks show a better NPL result than the whole banking sector with a NPL ratio of 1% by the end of 2012. NPLs of commercial banks concentrated in sectors like manufacturing with RMB 177.07 billion NPLs, wholesale and retail trade with RMB 107.14 billion NPLs, personal loans with RMB 48.73 billion NPLs and real estate with RMB 27.91 billion NPLs by the end of 2012 (CBRC 2013b: 171).

Figure 3-4: NPLs of commercial banks from 2005 to 2012

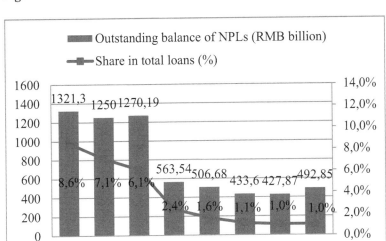

Source: CBRC 2012a: 32&124/CBRC 2006e/CBRC 2013b: 169

Loan loss provision ratio of commercial banks has increased from 41.4% in 2007 to 295.5% in 2012 (see Table 3-18). Since 2008 the loan loss provision ratio of commercial banks has exceeded 100%. Adequate funds were set aside to cover loan losses.

Table 3-18: Loan loss provision coverage ratio of commercial banks from 2007 to 2012

Item/Year	2007	2008	2009	2010	2011	2012
Loan loss provision coverage ratio	41.4%	116.6%	153.2%	217.7%	278.1%	295.5%

Source: CBRC 2013b: 169

Because loan business is the most important business of a banking institution, management of credit risk is of vital importance. These indicators have the ability to give warning signals of credit risks from different perspectives. However, the most essential issues for loan management are sound internal control system, sound credit policies and procedures, effective organizational structure for credit management, separation of loan approval from loan release, sound documentation system and sound information management system inside banking institutions (PBC 2001).

3.3.4 Supervision on profitability risk

Profitability situation is an important signal for the sustainability of a banking institution and it also belongs to important supervisory item. Profitability will not only be illustrated by the real profits of a financial institution, but also measured by the return on equity (ROE) and return on assets (ROA). They're the most common accounting-based performance measures. Both of the two indicators are used by Chinese authority for the overall evaluation of financial institutions. The ROE measures only the return on assets of the equity owners, while the ROA aggregates the return of equityholders and debtholders (Groß 2007: 26). The calculation methods of the two indicators are introduced below:

$$\text{ROE} = \frac{\text{net profit}}{\text{shareholders' equity}} \geq 11\% \text{ (CBRC 2005d)}$$

$$\text{ROA} = \frac{\text{net profit}}{\text{total assets}} \geq 0.6\% \text{ (CBRC 2005d)}$$

As we know, value of net profit cannot really show the performance of a banking institution, because it does not adjust to the bank's size. ROA measures a firm's efficiency at generating profits from every unit of assets. The minimum requirement of 0.6% was regulated in the "Core indicators for risk-based supervision of commercial banks" in 2005. ROE is net income divided by shareholders' equity and it measures a firm's efficiency at generating profits from every unit of shareholders' equity. It shows how well a company uses investment funds to generate earnings. ROE of commercial banks should be no less than 11% according to the CBRC regulation in 2005 (CBRC 2005d).

The total banking sector has experienced profit increase from 2007 to 2011. The profit volume after tax has tripled itself and by the end of 2011 the profit volume after tax reached RMB 1251.87 billion (see Table 3-20). The growth in profitability was mainly attributed to the increase in the size of interest-bearing credit assets, the rise in banking operational efficiency, improvement in credit risk management and the continuously stable interest spread.

Table 3-19: Profits after tax of banking institutions from 2007 to 2011

Unit: RMB billion

Institutions/Year	2007	2008	2009	2010	2011
Total	**446.73**	**583.36**	**668.42**	**899.09**	**1251.87**
Policy banks & China Development Bank	48.93	22.98	35.25	41.52	53.67
Large commercial banks	246.60	354.22	400.12	515.12	664.66
JSCBs	56.44	84.14	92.50	135.80	200.50
City commercial banks	24.81	40.79	49.65	76.98	108.09
UCCs	0.77	0.62	0.19	0.01	0.02
RCBs	4.28	7.32	14.9	27.9	51.22
RcoBs	5.45	10.36	13.49	17.90	18.19
RCCs	19.34	21.91	22.79	23.29	53.12
New-type rural financial institutions & Postal savings bank	0.65	0.65	3.22	11.90	25.79

Source: CBRC 2012a: 122

The development of ROA and ROE of whole banking sector is not as tremendous as the net profit amount. ROA of all banking institutions increased from 0.9% in 2007 to 1.2% in 2012, while ROE of all banking institutions rose from 16.7% in 2007 to 19.0% in 2012 (see Table 3-20). We can interpret from the moderate development of ROA and ROE that assets and equity of banking sector have also enlarged themselves enormously in this period. Both ROA and ROE have fulfilled the requirements set by CBRC in 2005.

Table 3-20:   Returns of banking institutions from 2007 to 2012

Unit: %

Items/Year	2007	2008	2009	2010	2011	2012
Banking institutions						
ROA	0.9	1.0	0.9	1.0	1.2	1.2
ROE	16.7	17.1	16.2	17.5	19.2	19.0
Commercial banks						
ROA	0.9	1.1	1.0	1.1	1.3	1.3
ROE	16.7	19.5	18.0	19.2	20.4	19.8

Source: CBRC 2012a: 123/CBRC 2013: 168

3.4   Summary

In this part, the main supervisory authorities, the legal framework for banking supervision and main supervisory indicators were introduced. After the establishment of the CBRC in 2003, we see great change of regulatory framework for the supervision of banking sector. The supervision has also developed to a risk-based supervisory work. There is less and less difference between the Chinese and international supervisory standards. In some perspectives the requirements for Chinese banking sector are more stringent than the international standards. From the data cited we can also conclude that the whole banking sector is overall robust in recent years.

Part III   **Overall RCC Situation and RCC Reform in China since 1996**

4.   History and performance of Rural Credit Cooperatives

As illustrated in the second part of this thesis, RCCs play a dominant role in the Chinese rural financial market. Not only do they have the largest network of financial branches in Chinese rural areas, particularly in townships and villages, they also have a long business history in the countryside. By the end of 2012, there were all together 74,707 branches of rural cooperative financial institutions including RCCs, RcoBs and RCBs with assets volume of RMB 15.5121 trillion (PBC 2013d: 2/CBRC 2013b: 164). By the end of 2012 the outstanding agriculture-related loans of rural cooperative financial institutions reaches RMB 5.3 trillion, which is 30% of total outstanding agriculture-related loans (CBRC 2013a). Among them RMB 2.7 trillion were loans extended to rural households, which accounted to 75.2% of total loans to rural households (CBRC 2013a). As I have concluded in the summary of chapter 2, rural cooperative financial institutions are the most important and irreplaceable RFIs in China, whose development will decide the financial supply in rural areas.

The analysis of RCCs begins with the introduction of RCC history and performance in the past 20 years. The introduction of RCC history will focus on the change of RCC numbers and governance structure, their cooperative constitution, the management and supervision authority of RCCs and their business from 1951 until now. As changes after 1996 will be specifically treated in subsequent chapters, the main focus of the introduction to RCC history will be on the period between 1951 and 1995.

In the part of performance illustration, only the latest developments can be shown statistically because of the inaccessibility of RCC data in the decades from the 1950s to the 1980s. The main indicators cited here have been introduced and explained in the third part (e.g. CAR, ratio of NPLs, ROE, ROA, etc.). This qualitative and quantitative analysis of RCCs' historical development and performance is the logical beginning for the further introduction of RCC reform in the last two decades. Furthermore, the reason for RCCs' reform can also be deducted based on the description of RCCs' business.

Upon the introduction of basic background of RCCs, the two important reform programs will be analyzed and evaluated in chapter 5 and chapter 6. The importance of RCCs for the Chinese rural financial market is undeniable, but the question of how to change them into profitable and sustainable RFIs remains to be determined. The two rounds of reform provide a partial answer. The first round of reform in 1996 restored the cooperative constitution to RCCs. In the second round of reform in 2003, more organizational possibilities for the transformation of RCCs were allowed. A trend of merger of RCCs at and below the county level and commercialization can be observed. Key issues and problems of RCCs will also be exposed through the analysis of these two rounds of reform. Except the description of the two rounds of RCC reform, representative cases will be used to illustrate the process and effect of the reform.

4.1   RCC development

In this part RCCs' institutional development, change of nature and their management authorities will be introduced. In China there are four practical administrative levels: province, prefecture, county and township. By the end of 2011, there were altogether 34 provincial level divisions, 332 prefectural level divisions, 2853 county level divisions and 40466 township and village level divisions (See Figure 4-1). We will use in the following text this administrative hierarchy to illustrate the institutional development of RCCs.

Figure 4-1:   Government administrative hierarchy in China by the end of 2011

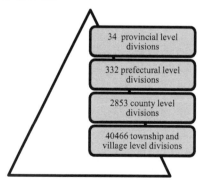

Source: http://baike.baidu.com/view/787783.htm

RCCs were originally a policy product. They were set up at the beginning at the same administrative levels as townships and villages. As indicated by their name, they should serve financial needs in Chinese rural areas with cooperative organization as their organizational form. The oldest RCC institutional structure was established at the township and village level in 1951 under the slogan "One village, one cooperative" and referred to as a "township-based RCC system". Although called a RCC system, these RCCs were at that time only tenuously connected. In this system, each township is equipped with one and only one RCC in most parts of China (Liu, Xu et al. 2005: 4). A RCC in one township could only have its members and clients from the local township and it could only run its business within its geographic boundaries. Trans-township financial business was not permitted. RCCs were ultimately managed and supervised by the PBC.

During this period, RCCs experienced great gross growth. By 1954, 124,000 RCCs had been established (Zhang et al. 2010: 17). By 1955, the number had increased to 159,000 (Zhang et al. 2010: 17). In 1956, the number decreased slightly to 103,000 because of administrative mergers of districts and townships (Zhang et al. 2010: 17). RCCs served as the only official financial institution at the lowest administrative level in the Chinese countryside.

Figure 4-2:   Development of RCCs' governance structure

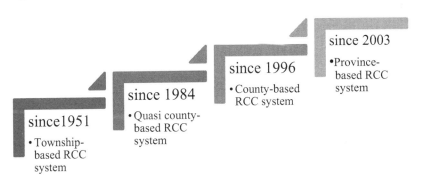

After the collectivization movement in 1959, RCCs were subordinated to people's communes[2]. The control rights were transferred downward to the local production brigades or village cadres (Ong 2006: 182). RCCs became a part of the brigades' finance bureaus, underlining the fact that the peasants had lost control over the cooperatives (Ong 2006: 182). The ownership of RCCs changed accordingly from private to collective ownership.

With the collapse of the commune system that previously controlled RCCs, the central government placed RCCs under the control of the state-owned ABC in 1979. Though effectively state-owned financial institutions, part of their capital was sourced from their members. The RCCs in China were initially scattered throughout townships and villages in rural China. With the transfer of its management into the hands of the ABC, RCCs operated on the existing network and structure of the ABC.

Figure 4-3:   Management right transfer of RCCs

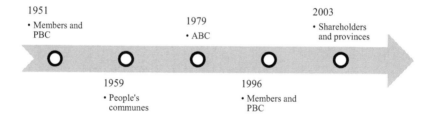

A two-level legal-person system of RCCs was established with the foundation of county RCC unions. The foundation of county RCC unions was initiated during the RCC reform between 1982 and 1984. The aim of this round of reform was to regulate the relationship between the ABC and RCCs. The original idea is that the ABC should no longer give orders to

---

2   During the twenty years from 1958 to 1978, peoples' communes made up the basic rural social and administrative units. There were 2000 to 4000 families in a people's commune, which combined for collective farming, fishing, mining, or industrial projects. They are also the highest among the three administrative levels in the countryside with production bridge and production teams at the second and third administrative levels.

RCCs but rather guide the business of RCCs. Instead of the ABC, county RCC unions should be established to take over the management work of township and village RCCs. According to the policy, the members' representative meeting would be reinstated and manager of RCCs should be elected by the members of RCCs. The county RCC unions and RCCs in townships and villages were given independent legal person status. County RCC unions had the tasks of management, coordination and pooling of funds for township RCCs. They even had the authority to appoint senior managers for township RCCs. 1,136 county RCC unions were established in this period (Wang 2009: 12). This reform trial of relationship regulation between the ABC and RCCs failed. RCCs kept controlled and managed by the ABC until 1996. But with the establishment of county RCC unions a "quasi county-based RCC system" was established.

In 1996, RCCs realized their independence through the official separation from the ABC. In the period between 1996 and 2003 RCCs tried to resume their cooperative nature and acted as independent financial institutions. County RCC unions could really fulfill their management tasks in this period. But county RCC unions and RCCs at the township and village level still had their independent legal person status.

In 2000, Jiangsu Province first tried to make breakthroughs of the old RCC system and clarified the relationship between county RCC unions and township RCCs. Counties in 11 cities in Jiangsu Provinces were chosen to merge township RCCs into county RCC unions in their region (Liu, Xu et al.2005: 7). Township RCCs and county RCC unions became one legal entity. 1,658 township RCCs and 82 county or city RCC unions have participated in the pilot program and were unified into 82 legal entities. In 2003, this unification trial was expended to eight pilot provinces. After one year, this reform method was implemented in other provinces in China. After the reform, county RCCs became the basic units of RCCs. Qualified areas could transform unified RCCs to RCBs or RcoBs. RCCs, RCBs and RcoBs all belong to rural cooperative financial institutions. The business operation of county RCCs is strictly confined to their corresponding administrative boundaries. Former RCCs at the township level with a good business record were preserved and became branches of county RCCs. Township branches of a county RCC could still only offer their financial services within their township boundaries.

According to the reform policy in 2003, provincial governments should take over the management right over RCCs. Hence, an umbrella organization above county RCCs was also set up, namely the provincial RCC union. Jiangsu Province established the first provincial RCC union in 2001. By the end of 2005, provincial RCC unions had been successfully established in 25 provinces and regions in China (Zhang et al. 2010: 94). In 2007, Hainan Province finished the last step of nationwide extension of provincial RCC unions. The establishment of provincial unions provided a platform for information sharing, legal consultation and other services. A province-based RCC system was then erected.

4.2   Financial performance of RCCs

Rural cooperative financial institutions have the largest network in Chinese rural areas among RFIs. Table 4-1 shows the development of the number of RCC, RCB and RcoB legal entities in counties and county-level cities from 2002 to 2010. The number of RCCs under the county level is not included. The total number of independent legal entities of rural cooperative financial institutions in counties and county-level cities changed very little from 2002 to 2010. Inside this group, however, we can observe a significant change overall in the number of different financial institutions. The number of unified county RCCs increased dramatically from only 94 in 2002 to 1976 in year 2010, while the number of county RCCs with separate legal status decreased accordingly from 2356 in 2002 to 132 in 2009 (see Table 4-1). This is the result of RCC reform which began officially in 2003. Most Chinese county RCCs merged with local RCCs under the county level into a single legal entity.

Table 4-1: Number of county RCCs, RcoBs and RCBs withseparate legal status from 2002 to 2010

Type of RFIs	2002	2003	2004	2005	2006	2007	2008	2009	2010
Two-level RCCs at the county level	2356	2345	2337	1832	1159	460	231	132	n.a.
Unified county RCCs	94	114	104	528	1201	1818	1973	1992	1976
RCBs	3	3	7	12	13	17	22	43	84
RcoBs	0	1	9	58	80	113	163	196	216
Sum	**2453**	**2463**	**2457**	**2430**	**2453**	**2408**	**2389**	**2363**	**n.a.**

Source: PBC 2011: 70

To illustrate the situation of RCCs more clearly, I will take the data of RFIs in 2009 as an example (see Table 4-2). The total amount of RCCs with separate legal status was 3,056; among them 1,992 were unified county RCCs and 132 were independent county RCCs (see Table 4-1/4-2). So there were 932 RCCs with independent legal status under the county level. The total amount of RCC branches reached 60,325 in 2009, one third more than the number of township level divisions of 40,466 in 2011 in China. When the staff number of RCCs is divided by the number of RCC branches, we find that each RCC branch has less than ten employees on average in 2009. In comparison with the number of clients, these cooperative financial institutions are inadequately staffed. The limited staffing hampers good service provision and also increases operational costs. A frequent area of criticism is that staff of RCCs is less qualified than staff in commercial banks.

Table 4-2: **Number of main RFIs and their branches by the end of 2009 and 2012**

RFIs/Year and items	End of 2009			End of 2012		
	Legal entity number	Branch number	Staff number	Legal entity number	Branch number	Staff number
Sum	3,467	75,935	715,216	3,274	75,896	809,733
RCCs	3,056	60,325	570,366	1,927	49,034	502,829
RCBs	43	7,259	66,317	337	19,910	220,042
RcoBs	196	8,134	74,776	147	5,463	55,822
VTBs	148	193	3,586	800	1,426	30,508
Lending companies	8	8	75	14	14	111
RMCC	n.a.	n.a.	n.a.	49	49	421
Others	16	16	96	0	0	0

Source: PBC 2011: 5/PBC 2013d: 2

Because of the limited official data and the late application of international evaluation methods, only the latest data of RCC performance is available. Table 4-3 shows the basic information of all RCCs nationwide from 1999 to 2010. It illustrates not only the scale of outstanding deposits and loans of RCCs, but also loan riskiness and profitability.

Table 4-3: **Main risk index of rural cooperative financial institutions from 1999 to 2010**

Unit: RMB billion and %

Year	Outstanding deposits	Outstanding loans	NPLs	NPL ratio	Net profit	Accumulative losses
1999	1335.8	922.6	472.6	51.23	-21.90	95.3
2000	1512.9	1048.9	517.4	49.00	-16.70	112.0
2001	1726.3	1197.1	526.7	44.00	-12.90	124.9
2002	1987.4	1393.7	514.7	36.93	-5.80	131.3
			514.7	36.93		
2003	2410.7	1719.4	508.4	29.57	-0.50	131.8
			506.0	29.45		
2004	2728.9	1923.8	444.4	23.10	10.46	121.3
			451.5	23.10		
2005	3257.3	2235.4	330.8	14.80	18.00	103.3
			325.5	14.80		
2006	n.a.	n.a.	303.3	11.56	n.a.	n.a.
2007	n.a.	n.a.	281.0	8.96	n.a.	n.a.
2008	n.a.	n.a.	296.5	7.96	n.a.	n.a.
2009	n.a.	n.a.	348.4	7.41	n.a.	n.a.
2010	8800.0 (PBC:9)	5900.0 (PBC:9)	318.3 (Mu)	5.60 (Mu)	67.80 (PBC:9)	n.a.

Source: Zhao 2008: 4/PBC 2011: 9& 70/Mu 2011: 15

Note:

This table is a combination of data from different reliable sources.

Data related to loans are calculated in the old loan classification method.

Data from 1999 to 2005 are sourced from Zhao's book "Study on running risk surveillance and early warning system of RCCs" and the PBC' publication "China rural finance service report 2010". The differences in the two sources are marked in two rows. In the upper row are data from Zhao and in the lower row are those from the PBC.

Data from 2006 to 2009 are from the same PBC's publication in 2011, page 70.

Data in 2010 are derived from Mu's book "Study on the legal person right and management system reform of RCCs" and the same PBC's publication in 2011, page 9.

From 1999 to 2010 the total amount of outstanding loans and outstanding deposits has experienced steady growth. From the table the most obvious change is the decrease of NPL ratio. The NPL ratio of RCCs decreased from 51.23% in 1999 to 5.6% in 2010. It should be mentioned that the data shown here were calculated in the old loan classification system. We can see clearly from Table 4-3 that the real amount of NPLs has sunk dramatically in 2004 and 2005. This volume has remained around RMB 300 billion since then. The significant decrease of the NPL ratio has to be ascribed to the fact that the denominator in the NPL ratio formula (the amount of loans) increased faster than the numerator (amount of NPLs). Although RCCs' outstanding loans increased almost triple between 2005 and 2010, the real amount of NPLs did not rise substantially in the old loan classification method. In the new loan classification method the volume of NPLs actually decreased from RMB 732.729 billion in 2006 to RMB 509.310 billion in 2009 (see Table 4-4). This can be seen as a proof of improvement of RCCs' control ability over credit risks.

Table 4-4: **Amount and ratio of NPLs in old and new loan classification system from 2006 to 2010**

Unit: RMB billion and %

Items/Year	2006	2007	2008	2009	2010
NPLs amount (old)	303.272	281.037	296.500	348.360	n.a.
NPLs amount (new)	732.729	659.597	593.895	509.310	n.a.
Ratio of NPLs (old)	11.50	8.96	7.96	7.41	5.60
Ratio of NPLs (new)	27.93	21.04	15.94	10.84	4.20
Loan loss provision coverage ratio (new)	8.18	14.38	24.11	36.98	n.a.

Source: PBC 2011: 70

Generally speaking, the asset situation of RCCs has not been optimistic. In 1999, more than half of the total number of loans extended by RCCs was bad. Moreover, the data of NPLs and CAR were calculated in the old loan classification method. This means that if the NPL ratio was recorded through the risk-based loan classification system the NPL ratio would be at least 5% higher than the stated amount in the table. This can be proved by the data in Table 4-4. We can see from the table that the ratio of NPLs of RCCs according to the risk-based loan classification method was still very high. In 2006, the ratio of NPLs reached 27.93%. In 2009, the indicator decreased to 10.84%, but only 36.98% of bad loans were covered by the loan loss provision, which was much lower than the required coverage ratio of 100% by the CBRC. High NPL ratio led causally to liquidity difficulties in these RCCs. After 2004, the volume of NPLs began to decline, which can be partly attributed to the financial support from the state to offset 50% of RCCs' NPLs during the RCCs' reform to improve assets quality of RCCs.

From the newest data of RCCs in 2010, we can observe a sizeable increase of outstanding deposits and loans of RCCs. The ratio of NPLs has also decreased to an acceptable level within 5%. The data here show very positive results for the latest situation of RCCs.

Table 4-5: **CAR of rural cooperative financial institutions in old and new loan classification method from 2002 to 2010**

Unit: %

Items/Year	2002	2003	2004	2005	2006	2007	2008	2009	2010
CAR in old method	-8.50	-9.01	-0.09	10.03	11.00	11.45	11.57		
CAR in new method						-0.10	3.47	6.00	8.70

Source: PBC 2011: 70

Besides the mountains of bad loans, severe historical losses of RCCs are another acute problem faced by RCCs. From Table 4-3 we can observe that the cumulative losses of RCCs increased from RMB 95.3 billion in 1999 to RMB 131.8 billion in 2003, which corresponded with the negative profit situation during these years. Actually RCCs had run losses in the ten consecutive years from 1994 to 2003 (Zhao 2008: 4). Since the capital situation was also negative during the time, most of the RCCs were bankrupt during these years. According to official estimates at the end of 2002, 19,542 RCCs, or 55 percent of them, had negative net worth or were technically bankrupt (Ong 2006: 178). The reform policy "Spend money to buy a new mechanism" during the reform in 2003 requires the participating RCCs to replenish their capital and increase the level of their CAR. CAR is a very important reference in determining whether special notes from the central bank can be cashed. This policy has shown very good effect. In 2005, CAR of RCCs in China increased from -0.9% to 10.03%.

Table 4-6: **Return on assets (ROA) of rural financial institutions from 2004 to 2006**

Unit: %

FIs/Year	2004	2005	2006
RCCs	0.16	0.29	0.42
RcoBs	0.61	0.84	1.01
RCBs	1.29	1.66	1.33
ABC	0.19	0.23	0.53

Source: Wang 2009: 30

Table 4-6 shows the ROA of rural cooperative financial institutions in comparison with the ABC. During the second round of reform, the return on assets ratio has duly increased for the listed rural financial institutions. RCBs earned the highest ROA in three consecutive years. RcoBs ranked as the second. RCCs on the other hand were far behind RcoBs and RCBs, but in the three recorded years, the probability of RCCs has also increased from 0.16% to 0.42%. The newly restructured RcoBs and RCBs are also proved to be profitable, and more profitable than RCCs and the ABC measured by the indicator ROA, which can guarantee a sustainable development of them in the future (see Table 4-6).

We can conclude from the data above that the scale of RCC business has been steadily increasing from 1999 to 2010. RCCs have historically accrued a large amount of NPLs and losses. In 1999, 51.23% loans of nationwide RCCs were non-performing with the real amount of RMB 472.6 million. In the last decade the situation of RCCs has improved itself in big step. The historical burdens of RCCs have been relieved, and their profitability and sustainability have improved. The reasons for the development will be explained in a detailed introduction to the two rounds of RCC reform.

5.   RCC reform in 1996

RCCs were established in 1951 as cooperative financial institutions owned by their members to serve the financial needs in rural areas. From 1959, RCCs belonged to village or township communes and were later turned into collective-owned institutions. The first task of RCCs at that time was to serve the financial needs of communes. After the ABC took over the management right of RCCs in 1979, RCCs were accorded nominal business independence but became ABC branches in some areas in reality. RCCs either merged with local ABC branches or were managed by the same ABC leaders of ABC branches (Shen et al. 2010: 312). To be ABC local branches means that RCCs did not realize their business independence and functioned as policy tools. In this process, we can observe that RCCs were confronted with severe unclear ownership. The other problem is that although RCCs are considered cooperative organizations, they realized their cooperative nature only in the early years.

The State has repeatedly attempted to solve the management problem of RCCs. RCC unions at the county level were established to manage RCCs independently in 1984. This independence was, however, very limited since these RCC unions were de facto divisions of the ABC county offices (Shen et al. 2010: 312). The unconventional marriage between the ABC and RCCs worked for almost 17 years. During this period, RCCs deviated from their cooperative development direction and failed to fulfill their mission of serving the financial needs of rural residents, while the ABC could not achieve its commercialization goals without getting rid of the management task of RCCs (State Council of the PRC 1996). Furthermore, RCCs have suffered bad performance for a long time. As we in Table 4-3 of the last chapter see, the NPL ratio of RCCs in 1999 reached 51.23%. Before 2004, RCCs had not made any profits for the previous 10 consecutive years (Zhao 2008: 4). Under this background newest round of RCC reform was initiated by the State Council in 1996.

5.1   Policy design of this round of RCC reform

The State Council promulgated the "Decision on rural financial system reform" in 1996, symbolizing the start of rural financial reform in China. This decision aimed at clarifying the relationship between main rural official financial institutions like the ABC, the ADBC and RCCs so that a multi-level financial system with commercial banks offering services to satisfy industrial and commercial needs, cooperative financial institutions, farmers and policy banks supporting the agricultural sector and promoting agricultural technology improvement could be established in rural areas. To further facilitate the division of work between different financial institutions, RCCs were decoupled from the ABC. With the further separation of the policy portfolio, the ABC became a SOCB. RCCs were to be reformed on a cooperative model, which should be held and managed democratically by their members who should be the primary beneficiaries of their services. This decision of the State Council was also seen as the beginning of reform of RCCs. In the following text, I will first give an introduction of reform methods aimed at RCCs and then analyze the results of this round of RCC reform.

The first goal of this round of RCC reform was for RCCs to be separated from the ABC. The decision gave guidance for the establishment of new management authorities of RCCs. The method used was to establish RCC unions at the county level to be responsible for the management and coordination of RCCs in this region. At the beginning of the reform, the management of RCCs was shifted to the newly established Inter-ministerial Coordination and Leading Group for Rural Financial Reforms in 1996. Later on, RCCs were managed by the county RCC unions in their respective administrative areas. There were two organizational forms of county RCC unions recommended by the State Council in this decision. They could be organized either in the form of an association financed by members' fees or as a shareholding financial entity with township RCCs in this region as their shareholders (State council of the PRC 1996). It was further stipulated in the decision that directors of county RCC unions should be elected by representatives of grassroots RCCs. The elected candidates should be reported to county branches of the PBC for first step qualification examination. After that, candidates should be reported to prefectural (city) branches of the PBC for approval (State Council of the PRC 1996). To make sure that county RCC unions could successfully take over the management function of RCCs, they would absorb qualified and experienced professionals from the ABC and grassroots RCCs into their newly established team (State Council of the PRC 1996). There was no data about the number of county RCC unions established during this period.

According to the "Provisions concerning management of county RCC unions" published by the PBC in 1997, county RCC unions should be responsible for funds transfer between underlining RCCs, clearing and settlement business of underlining RCCs on their commission, management of syndicated loans, collection and management of risk provisions of RCCs (PBC 1997b).

Another issue needing clarification was the supervision issue of RCCs. The decision regulated that PBC county branches should be responsible for the supervision work of RCCs at the county level. A vice president of a PBC county branch should be appointed to be responsible for the supervision work of RCCs (State Council of the PRC 1996). The supervisory efforts focus mainly on institutional establishment, interest rate management, risk management, financial service guidance and personnel qualification examination. PBC county branch can also recruit experienced professionals from the ABC to support their supervisory work. Deposit reserves of RCCs saved in the ABC should also be transferred accordingly to the PBC.

After the framework for the management and supervision of RCCs is established, the task of restructuring of RCCs as cooperative organizations could begin. The PBC republished the "Administrative provisions on RCCs" in 1997 as reference for the building up of RCCs' cooperative nature. In this document, ownership structure, democratic management and service design of RCCs were redefined. For accounting issues, RCCs should consult the "Accounting system for financial and insurance enterprises" promulgated by the Ministry of Finance. The first task in the restructuring of RCCs was to enlarge the group of shareholders. The target group would be made up of rural residents, rural collective enterprises and RCC employees. Second, a democratic corporate structure should be set up according to the requirements of a cooperative organization with the members' representative meeting as the highest decision-making organ. In this meeting, each representative would have only one vote. The board of directors and board of supervisors should fulfill their functions properly. The third task was to define the direction of RCCs' services. The services of RCCs should be oriented towards the members' needs. Loans disbursed to members should make up at least 50% of total loan volume of RCCs.

Loan applications for farming and breeding industry would enjoy the priority according to the decision (State Council of the PRC 1996).

In some developed regions with high level of urban-rural integration, rural cooperative banks (RcoBs) could be set up in counties and county-level cities instead of RCCs. RcoBs are viewed as a more advanced form of organization than RCCs (State council of the PRC 1996). The precondition is that these RCCs should already operate their business commercially. RcoBs are commercial banks and should operate according to the requirements in the "Law of the People's Republic of China on commercial banks". The minimum initial capital should be at least RMB 50 million with county or city government, enterprises and residents as their shareholders (State council of the PRC 1996). If RCCs choose to merge with RcoBs, they must give up their legal status and operate as branches of new established RcoBs. Urban credit cooperatives can also integrate into RcoBs in the same way. This means RcoBs can only be organized as one legal entity. RcoBs would serve mainly agricultural, processing of agricultural products and other agriculture-related branches according to the decision (State council of the PRC 1996).

The decision imposed a time table for reform. By the second half of 1996, county RCC unions and PBC county branches were required to have already enlarged and enriched their management and supervision team and the separation work should be completed so that the restructuring of RCCs could begin (State council of the PRC 1996). In the second half of 1996, each province (autonomous region and municipality) was to choose one or two economically developed counties to launch a pilot project of RcoBs that would be approved by the PBC after the examination by the Inter-ministerial Coordination and Leading Group for Rural Financial Reforms (State council of PRC 1996).

5.2 Results and overall evaluation of this round of reform

The upshot of this round of reform is that RCCs were completely separated from the ABC. A two-level management structure with a county RCC union at the upper level and township RCCs at the under level was established. As a consequence of the separation from the ABC, bad assets of RCCs increased due to their inheritance from the ABC after the break. So the ABC enjoyed an optimistic balance sheet with the separation of bad assets from its account. After the rural co-operative foundation (RCF) closed in 1998, bad debts left by the RCF were also transferred to RCCs. By the end of 1999, the ratio of NPLs reached 51.23% (see Table 4-3). Furthermore, RCCs were treated adversely as the reform policy favored commercialization of the ABC. RCCs were appointed to be responsible for financial business of small-scale credits with high risk, while the ABC was responsible for large credit clients with relatively low risk. As it were, the reform brought numerous new challenges to RCCs. From the skeletal policy content we can safely surmise that no mature considerations were made about the future of RCCs. RCCs were like scapegoats, bearing the sins of the ABC and the RCF and generating favorable conditions for the ABC commercialization. They were left with risky clients and bad assets. No reprieve on tax liability, financial subsidies or policy support was given to the related RCCs (Wang / Gao 2009: 28). But the fact that RCCs were still under the supervision and management of the PBC meant that they could still carry out their policy tasks with help from the State.

Although the reform program required RCCs to absorb rural residents and enterprises into their shareholder group, critics charge that the reform policy did not clarify the ownership of the already existing capital of RCCs and failed to identify the owners of newly collected capital; so the property right of each RCC member could not be guaranteed (Wang / Gao 2009: 27). This problem of unclear ownership became especially acute for RCCs after their separation from the ABC.

Researcher Zhengrong Mu of the PBC commented in his book about corporate governance of RCCs. In his opinion, corporate RCCs could not fulfill the cooperative requirements of democratic management after the separation with the ABC in 1996 (Mu 2011: 40). The first reason he offered is that the ownership structure of RCCs is too dispersed. In order to reach the required RCCs' lowest level of capital of RMB 1 million (PBC 1997a), RCCs tried to enlarge their membership to increase their capital volume. According to the "Administrative provisions on RCCs" each individual member cannot share more than 2% of total shares (PBC 1997a). This leads to a more fragmented and dispersed ownership structure of RCCs. Because of their limited access to shares, shareholders have little incentive to exercise their power. Second, shareholders have the freedom to withdraw their shares when the business situation of RCCs gets worse. They do not really need to worry about losses because of the low profitability of RCCs. Third, rural residents and farmers as the main members of RCCs have no management ability to engage in the decision-making of RCCs' big issues because of their low education level (Mu 2011: 40). The management right of RCCs lies in the hands of "insiders" (i.e. employee shareholders) in reality, Mu observed (Mu 2011: 40). Although a corporate structure with decision-making organs has been established in RCCs, it cannot be effective without shareholders taking a part in it.

A report of International Fund for Agricultural Development (IFAD) shared a similar assessment to the change of RCCs after this round of reform. The report argues that efforts are being made to turn the RCCs into real cooperative banks, but these efforts have been unsuccessful so far (IFAD 2001: 44). "The same staff, who managed the RCC while it was under the ABC, now manages the county RCC unions." (IFAD 2001: 44) The names of these departments have changed but the management system and customs remain the same.

Detailed information about RCCs' equity situation, shareholding structure, asset quality and corporate governance after the separation unfortunately has not been made available. It has never been reported whether the goal of resume cooperative nature back to RCCs set in the decision was fully realized or not. Scientific evaluation reports about this round reform cannot be found making the analysis of this round of reform even more difficult. Only a few direct comments of some researchers mentioned above can be found to shed light on the results of this round of reform.

The "Decision on rural financial system reform" can be seen as the first step of RCC reform. Although many intrinsic problems of RCCs could not be solved overnight, the reform at least gave RCCs independent status as financial institutions. This is a very important platform of departure for further reform. But still the results of this round of reform are overall not so satisfying. Although RCCs were artificially separated from the ABC, they were left with more tasks and very bad asset situation. The management system stayed still under insiders' control.

This policy, like other policies in China, proceeds from top down and unnaturally severed the relationship between the ABC and RCCs in favor of the commercialization of the ABC. RCCs took on the responsibility alone for supplying rural financial services in Chinese rural area. Placing one of the only formal financial institutions in rural China with bad performance for an extended period of time in this position was a very risky proposal.

RCCs needed time to get used to being sustainable and independent. Furthermore, the policy is yet another example of the "one size fits all" policies in China. The further reform steps should take regional differences of RCCs' development into consideration and give more options for RCCs' restructuring. To solve open questions about the real implementation of democratic management and about the unclear ownership structure a further reform was urgently needed.

6. RCC reform since 2003

Although RCCs were artificially separated from the ABC, they were left with more tasks and a very bad asset situation. Inherent problems like unclear ownership, unrealized democratic management and corporate governance and insider control still exist. In this background, the second round of RCC reform was commenced. The initiative was based on experiences from a RCC reform trial in Jiangsu Province. In contrast with the first round reform this round of reform was carried out more cautiously. Besides the trial in the economically developed Jiangsu Province in 2000, the policy has also been tested in eight representative provinces and municipalities in China in the second half of 2003. It was not until the second half of 2004 that this reform was officially carried out in the other 21 provinces and municipalities.

Box 6-1:   **RCC reform trial in Jiangsu Province in 2000**

Jiangsu province near the Yangtse River is a well-developed and wealthy province in China and has clear advantages in meeting the preconditions for a reform trial. This province, which takes up only 1.1% of Chinese total area, made up of 10.4% of China' whole GDP by the end of 2011 (Statistics Bureau of Jiangsu Province 2012). From 1979 to 2011 its average growth rate pro year reaches 12.6% (Statistics Bureau of Jiangsu Province 2012). The annual per capital GDP is RMB 27,207 higher than the average level in China according to the statistics in 2011 (Statistics Bureau of Jiangsu Province 2012). Because of its better economic situation Jiangsu Province is chosen as the first province to implement RCC reform.

Jiangsu Province put forward a proposal that the majority of its RCCs would be transformed into independent financial institutions responsible for their own risks and development over a period of 3 to 5 years (Chen 2004: 340). In July 2000, the State Council approved the reform plan, which was drafted by the PBC and the People's Government of Jiangsu Province together. The pilot reform of RCCs in Jiangsu began in August 2000 (Chen 2004: 340). The objective of this trial is that after conducting a general inventory of assets and clarifying the claims and liabilities situation, RCCs within a county (or county-level city) should merge into a single corporate entity (Chen 2004: 340). Mandate of this pilot trial was to "perfect RCC structure, transform their mechanism, resolve the problem of excessive burdens, strengthen RCCs' management and improve their services" (Chen 2004: 340). With this reform, 1658 grass-root RCCs and 82 county RCC unions were merged into 82 cooperate entities in Jiangsu. Capabilities of operational management and risk-bearing were improved through the merger. Furthermore, a provincial RCC union was set up to manage all county RCCs at the provincial level in September 2001 (Chen 2004: 341). This is a process of restructuring RCC system. Former dispersed small township and village RCCs merged together to a county-wide financial institution. The management of RCCs was also transferred into the hands of provincial RCC union.

The reform trial didn't stop with the merger process. Jiangsu Province tried to further transform RCCs into JSCBs in advanced areas. In three municipalities Zhangjiagang, Changshu and Jiangyin, RCCs were reorganized into joint-stock commercial banks, which are named as rural commercial banks (RCBs). The successful commercial trial in these three cities proved the feasibility of this organizational form for economically advanced areas and then the idea was introduced in the reform policy.

We first have a look at the policy framework of this round RCC reform. Building on the experiences of Jiangsu Province, the 2002 National Financial Working Conference laid down the basic principles of RCC reform (Zhang et al. 2010: 27). The conference decided that the one-size-fits-all organizational patterns are ineffective; commercialization should be allowed in qualified regions; management should not be vertical across the country; microcredit should be continued; and provincial government should participate in risk mitigation (Zhang et al. 2010: 27). In June 2003, the State Council published "Scheme for deepening the pilot reform of Rural Credit Cooperatives" (the 15th document of the State Council in 2003) in order to launch the pilot RCC reform in first eight provinces. To guide further reform, the State Council published "Opinions on further deepening the pilot reform of Rural Credit Cooperatives" in 2004 and applied the further enlargement of the reform areas to 21 other provinces and municipalities. These two documents from the State Council were hailed as invaluable guidance for this round of RCC reform. The CBRC also released more detailed regulations to support the implementation of RCC reform (see Table 6-1). These regulations give clear definitions and requirements for the new organizational forms like Rural Commercial Banks (RCBs), Rural Cooperative Banks (RcoBs), and unified county (or city) RCCs. Table 6-1 broadly lists the most important documents and notices from the State Council and the CBRC to give a policy overview. These documents will be partly introduced as the policy basis in the following text.

Table 6-1: **RCC reform policies and supporting regulations**

Guidance of RCC reform in 2003 from the State Council	Scheme for deepening the pilot reform of Rural Credit Cooperatives / The 15th document of the State Council in 2003(June 2003)
	Opinions on further deepening the pilot reform of Rural Credit Cooperatives (August 2004)
Supporting regulations from the CBRC	Interim provisions concerning management of rural commercial banks (2003)
	Interim provisions concerning management of rural cooperative banks (2003)
	Guidelines of the CBRC concerning the unification work of RCCs' legal person with county and city as basic unit (2003)
	Interim provisions concerning management of RCC unions in provinces (autonomous regions and municipalities directly under the central government) (2003)
	Several opinions of the CBRC on regulating purchase of shares of rural cooperative financial institutions (2004)

The next section introduces the content of the most important reform policy, the "Scheme for deepening the pilot reform of Rural Credit Cooperatives", so that the guidelines of this round of reform can be framed out. After that the implementation of each important item will be verified separately to give a deep insight into the core of this round of reform and finally an evaluation of this round of reform will be presented.

6.1 Reform policy of the State Council's 15th document

In this part starting point of this round RCC reform namely the 15th document of the State Council will be introduced. In this document, the State Council appealed to all RCCs to accelerate their management system reform and ownership transformation. The reform should be implemented following the main spirit **"clarify RCCs' property right, strengthen their control mechanism, improve RCCs' service functions, provide appropriate support from the State, and delegate responsibility to local governments"**. The objective is to transform RCCs into true community financial institutions (owned by farmers, rural enterprises and various rural economic organizations) providing services to Sannong – also known as the Three Rural Issues, namely agriculture, rural areas, and peasants.

Two main issues to be dealt with in further deepening RCC reform are ownership transformation to improve corporate governance through various ownership structures and restructuring the managerial regime with the objective of delegating RCC management to local governments (Xie et al. 2005: 46). The main part of the pilot scheme in 2003 will be reformulated in the following part, to keep its authenticity arranged so as to correspond with of the first three policies is the same as presented in the original document.

6.1.1 RCCs' ownership transformation

The first issue of this round of RCC reform is to solve the problem of unclear ownership of RCCs. Before the ownership can be clarified, RCCs' current assets and liabilities situation must be verified.

For RCCs with positive net worth, the surplus should first of all be distributed as dividends to their shareholders and be used to pay back unpaid interest and various insurance premiums (Xie et al. 2005: 46/State Council of the PRC 2003). The remainder should be set aside as loan loss provisions, which can only be counted as subsidiary capital (Xie et al. 2005: 46/State Council of the PRC 2003). The volume of loan loss provisions should be calculated according to the risk level of assets. Since RCCs at that time were still using the old loan classification system, loans were categorized into pass, overdue, idle and bad. RCCs should set aside capital at 1% of pass loans, 20% of overdue loans, 50% of idle loans and 100% of bad loans as loan loss provisions to meet possible loan risks (Xie et al. 2005: 46/State Council of the PRC 2003). The remaining funds may be used to bolster capital base (Xie et al. 2005: 46/State Council of the PRC 2003).

For insolvent RCCs which cannot be shut down now, their remaining earnings should be used to offset accumulated losses. The remaining losses should be cleared up in the future process of RCCs' institutional restructuring, management improvement and policy support.

After the assets and liabilities situation of RCCs is clarified, the next steps of the pilot reform come: ownership structure should be privatized, new organizational forms should be introduced for RCCs' restructure, and corporate governance should be improved accordingly. The pilot scheme of the State Council provides for the pilot regions various legal structures based on local circumstances. "In localities where conditions permit, RCCs shall be transformed into joint-stock banks; in those localities where conditions are not adequate, cooperative joint-stock banks shall be tested; in those localities where conditions are appropriate for cooperatives but not for joint-stock companies, then cooperatives shall be tried." (Xie et al. 2005: 46/State Council of the PRC 2003) Three kinds of legal entities and two disposal possibilities of high risk and insolvent RCCs are defined in the pilot scheme and are here listed in Table 6-2.

Table 6-2: **Possibilities and requirements for RCCs'**
transformation in the pilot scheme

Joint-stock banks	In advanced localities with a high degree of urbanization, joint-stock banks shall be established based on the RCCs if they are sufficiently large and commercially oriented. Specific criteria include: Management is strong; Total assets exceed RMB 1 billion; NPL ratio is below 15%; Initial capital after restructuring exceeds RMB 50 million and CAR reaches 8%.
Unified county RCCs	In densely populated localities or prefectures/ municipalities/counties designated as grain or cotton production bases, RCCs and RCC unions shall be consolidated into a unified legal entity. Specific criteria include: Positive net worth on consolidated basis; Consent by grassroots level RCCs; Relatively strong management at the RCC union; Capital after ownership consolidation exceeds RMB 10 million, and CAR reaches specified ratios.
RCCs and county RCC unions as independent legal entities	In other localities, the current two-tier system where RCCs and RCC unions are both legal entities shall be continued to make them better cooperatives.
Shutdown or merger	For highly risky RCCs effective measures should be used to accelerate merger and acquisition. Those deeply insolvent RCCs located in urban or peri-urban areas can be shut down according to the "Regulations on withdrawal of financial institutions".

Source: Xie et al. 2005: 46-47

6.1.2 Transfer of RCCs' management to local government

After RCCs separated from the ABC, a county RCC union took over the management right over local township RCCs. The whole RCC system was actually managed by the PBC. The PBC has been criticized for its double role as manager and regulator. In this pilot scheme, it has defined the change of management of RCCs clearly as the second important issue for this round of RCC reform. RCCs will have more regional features through the transfer of management rights to the provincial government. The tasks of the provincial government include:

1. The provincial government will make sure RCCs comply with financial policies and guidelines set by the State and will guide their operations in the direction of serving Sannong (State Council of the PRC 2003). Local party committees shall set up their leadership over RCC party membership and is responsible for ideological work (Xie et al. 2005: 47).

2. The provincial government will "provide guidance to RCCs in accordance with laws and regulations to strengthen their self-discipline and supervise the election and appointment of RCC senior managers in accordance with laws and regulations" (Xie et al. 2005: 47).

3. The provincial government will take the responsibility of preventing and resolving financial risks of RCCs in its jurisdiction (Xie et al. 2005: 47). The central bank can only provide temporary financial support to highly risky RCCs, when the provincial government permits fiscal authorities to withhold future transfer payment from central government to the provincial government should it fail to repay the central bank loans (Xie et al. 2005: 47).

4. "The provincial government will assist RCCs in collecting old loans and in fighting willful default, in investigating and punishing fraud, and in creating a healthy credit culture and maintaining order and stability in rural finance." (Xie et al. 2005: 47)

In pilot areas where conditions are appropriate, a provincial RCC union or other forms of provincial management organs can be established at the provincial level, which should take the responsibility of managing, guiding, coordinating and serving local RCCs under the leadership of the provincial government. The management right cannot be appropriated by lower-level governments. Under the provincial level, no other RCC unions or other forms of independent units should be established (Xie et al. 2005: 47). The provincial government should not intervene in the concrete business operations of RCCs; it only occupies the management role at the macro-level.

It's further regulated in the pilot scheme that the CBRC as the national banking supervisory authority should also fulfill its corresponding supervisory duty over RCCs. Its main responsibilities include:

"1. Formulating supervisory regulations over RCCs in accordance with State laws and regulations;

2. Checking and approving the establishment, changes, termination and business scope of banking institutions;

3. Conducting on-site examinations and off-site surveillance, collecting statistical information and conducting risk evaluation as well as investigating and penalizing illegal acts of RCCs;

4. Conducting fit-and-proper tests of senior managers;

5. Providing provincial government with collected data and statistics, early warning on risky institutions and assisting provincial governments in dealing with risks;

6. Providing training to specialized managerial staff of provincial government;

7. Evaluating performance of provincial government in managing RCCs and reporting findings to the State Council." (Xie et al. 2005: 48/State Council of the PRC 2003)

6.1.3 Reform supporting policies

Unlike the first round of reform, the central government will provide fiscal support, tax reduction and exemption, and central government funds in order to facilitate absorption of losses from the past and pave the way for the smooth implementation of the pilot project. The support content is listed below:

1. Fiscal subsidies from the Ministry of Finance to compensate losses caused by inflation-indexed deposits in RCCs during 1994-1997 (State Council of the PRC 2003). The amount of interest losses in RCCs shall be verified and reimbursed in stages (State Council of the PRC 2003).

2. From January 1, 2003 to December 31, 2005, income tax shall be canceled for all participating RCCs in the western region; it shall be halved for participating RCCs in other areas (Xie et al. 2005: 48). Business tax shall be collected at 3% for all participating RCCs in all pilot areas starting January 1, 2003 (State Council of the PRC 2003). In 2006, the tax reduction and exemption for RCCs was extended for another 3 years (Zhang et al 2010: 94). The first 8 pilot provinces and regions can enjoy the tax policy until end of 2008, the other 21 provinces and municipalities entering the reform in 2004 can be covered by the policy until end of 2009.

3. Two options of financial support from the central bank are available for RCCs in pilot regions. The first option is special lending from the PBC in worth of 50% of total negative net worth (insolvency amount) of these RCCs calculated at the end of 2002 (State Council of the PRC 2003). The interest rate of the special lending should be half of the interest rate of required reserves at the central bank (State Council of the PRC 2003). The maturities of special lending are set at 3, 5 and 8

years (State Council of the PRC 2003). In this case provincial governments are the units to apply for special lending according to the amount of the negative net worth of all RCCs in this province (State Council of the PRC 2003). The funds will be managed and repaid by provincial governments.

Negative net worth is defined as the following formula

Negative net worth = cumulative losses + actual asset loss − owner's equity − loan loss reserves

Actual asset loss = bad loans + idle loans × 40% + overdue loans × 10% + investment × 10% + foreclosed loans × 50%

The other option to get the central banks' funding is to apply for special 2-year notes issued by the PBC also at 50% of negative net worth (insolvency amount) used to exchange NPLs of RCCs (State Council of the PRC 2003). The interest rate of special notes should not be lower than that of required reserves at the central bank (Xie et al. 2005: 49). These special notes cannot be traded, endorsed or used as collateral (Xie et al. 2005: 49). They can be redeemed ahead of maturity under a few conditions. The disbursement of special notes will depend on the reform performance of participating RCCs. The criteria for disbursement of special notes include clear ownership structure, paid-up capital and good corporate governance (Xie et al. 2005: 49). County RCCs are the basic units to apply for special notes. The local branches of the PBC and the CBRC as well as local governments will monitor if RCCs satisfy the criteria. Participating localities shall be free to choose an option based on its actual situation or adopt "one province, two systems" provided that the total amount didn't exceed 50% of actual insolvency amount as of end 2002 (Cai 2010b: 137).

4. In those areas where informal finance is prevalent, more flexible interest rates are allowed in RCCs in these regions (Xie et al. 2005: 49). Lending rates can float between 1 and 2 times the benchmark lending rate set by the PBC (Xie et al. 2005: 49). Lending rate for microcredit loans to farmers on the other side shall not float upwards except in rare cases of high risk micro loans (Xie et al. 2005: 49). The lending rate of microcredit loans still should not be more than 1.2 times that of regulated rates (Xie et al. 2005: 49). In areas afflicted with natural disasters lending rates to farming households can be floated downwards to the appropriate level (Xie et al. 2005: 49).

6.1.4 The pilot areas in 2003 and 2004

The pilot to deepen RCC reform shall be organized and implemented by the CBRC according to the scheme of the State Council (Xie et al 2005: 49). Provincial/municipal government can apply to participate in the pilot scheme on a voluntary basis. Applications will be screened by the CBRC and should be submitted to the State Council for approval. Only 3-5 provinces from the eastern, central and western parts of China shall be selected under the 2003 pilot scheme (Xie et al 2005: 49).

But in reality eight regions comprising Jilin, Shandong, Shanxi, Jiangsu, Zhejiang, Jiangxi, Guizhou provinces and Chongqing Municipality passed the final approval for the initial implementation of the pilot. These regions are marked in blue color in the following map. The regions chosen reflect considerable regional differences in China. Jiangsu, Zhejiang and Shandong represent wealthy eastern coastal regions with high devclopment levels. Shanxi, Guizhou and Chongqing represent the western part of China with below average development levels. Jilin in Northeast and Jiangxi in the middle of the country are two big agricultural provinces. First experiences should be gained first from these districts with strong regional characteristics. Efforts will be made to experiment managerial regime change and test ownership transformation methods.

Figure 6-1: **Select provinces and city for the first round of reform in 2003**

A year later, the RCC reform was extended to the remaining 21 regions of China including the three centrally administered municipalities of Beijing, Tianjin, Shanghai and the provinces of Hebei, Shanxi, Inner Mongolia Autonomous Region, Liaoning, Heilongjiang, Anhui, Fujian, Henan, Hubei, Hunan, Guangdong, Guangxi, Sichuan, Yunnan, Gansu, Ningxia Hui Autonomous Region, Qinghai and Xinjiang Uyghur Autonomous Region

(State Council of the PRC 2004). The only regions not included in the RCC reform were the Tibet Autonomous Region and Hainan Province.

6.2   Scale, conditions, aim and results of financial supporting measures

A noteworthy characteristic of this round of reform was that this time a large amount of financial support was offered by the state. The whole concept behind it was to buy a robust mechanism through conditioned funds; the slogan of the concept can be pithily summarized as "Spend money to buy a new mechanism". First of all, this money was mainly used to relieve operational losses and NPLs of these RCCs so that the first barrier to the realization of a robust mechanism could be removed. Furthermore, conditions attached to monetary assistance such as capital replenishment and asset quality improvement simultaneously helped to fulfill the requirements of a robust mechanism. The best reflection of this concept is the third supporting policy from the PBC, the only one with conditions among the four policies. Additionally, the funding available in this policy is the greatest in comparison with the other 3 policies.

Let us first have a look at the available data of funding volume of these supporting policies. RMB 8.8 billion were granted to RCCs used as interest subsidies for RCCs' losses caused by indexed loans from 1994 to 1997 (Mu 2011: 5). The interest subsidies were distributed for duration of three years. RMB 76 billion income tax and business tax were eliminated by the end of 2010 (Mu 2011: 15). Funding from the central bank in the form of special notes or special lending amounted to RMB 171.8 billion by the end of 2010 (Mu 2011: 15). RMB 169.9 billion of that sum was granted in the form of special notes. Special lending on the other side totaled only RMB 1.9 billion (Mu 2011:15). Three provinces including Xinjiang Province have applied for and favored from the special lending (Mu 2011:15). Summing up the supporting funds mentioned above, altogether RMB 256.6 billion funds were granted to RCCs to relieve their historical burdens, which equals to over 80% of the negative net worth of all RCCs by the end of 2002 (Mu 2011: 15).

Table 6-3: **Amount of financial support for the RCC reform by the end of 2010**

Unit: RMB billion

Interest subsidies	8.8
Income tax and business tax	76.0
Special notes	169.9
special lending	1.9
Sum	256.6

Source: Mu 2011: 15

An innovation of funds support in this round of reform is that support is closely integrated into the reform process in the design of issuance and payment conditions and evaluation procedures of the funds so that the policy effect of "Spend money to buy a new mechanism" can be achieved (Cai 2010b: 137). Because the volume of special notes far exceeded the volume of special lending (see Table 6-3), we'll first look as the procedure and conditions to get special notes issued and disbursed.

The two-year special notes, which are seen as an extraordinary financial innovation (Cai 2010b: 139), were designed to be issued and cashed out to the RCCs in pilot regions to displace their NPLs and accumulative losses. The basic units for the application and evaluation are counties. The application procedure is very complicated. First of all, an application has to be screened by the CRBC and the PBC not only at the county but also at the provincial level. Secondly, when ratio of debt-equity gap to assets of RCCs in a county exceeds 20%, the application even must be turned over to CBRC and PBC headquarters in Beijing for approval.

The most important document for successful application of special notes is an equity replenishment plan, which should include a detailed plan of these participating RCCs in this county to increase their equity, enlarge the scale of shares and increase CAR as well as a plan to decrease NPLs using the special notes. Other important check points are listed below:

1. Regulatory compliance of equity enlargement including the compliance of qualification of investors or shareholders. Examples of special requirements for the enlargement of shares are no non-cash paid shares, no shares guaranteed with fixed interest rates as dividends, no shares purchased through RCC granted loans, no shares purchased by governmental organizations (Mu 2011: 9).

2. Regulatory compliance and accountability of the amount of the reported CAR and the goals set to increase RCCs' CAR. Lowest level for CAR after the displacement of NPLs and accumulative losses through supporting funds is set as 0% for RCCs with separate legal status at and under the county level, 2% for RCCs as unified entities at and under the county level and 8% for RCBs and RcoBs (Mu 2011: 9).

3. The order of displacement using special notes. The cashed out funds should be used first of all to displace bad loans and the remainder for idle loans, accumulative losses and other types of non-performing loans and assets. The order cannot be altered (Mu 2011: 9). The amount of special notes used to displace NPLs should not be lower than 65%. RCCs which did not merge with county RCCs and remained independent legal entities will receive special notes from the county RCCs in their region (Mu 2011: 9).

Once special notes are approved and issued by the central bank, they are actually liabilities for the central bank and risk-free assets for RCCs (Cai 2010b: 139). Before special notes are cashed out, RCCs holding central bank special notes can accrue 1.89% interest paid on a quarterly base (Xie et al. 2006: 32).

After a waiting period of two years, RCCs are allowed to apply for special notes' payment. RCCs that have fulfilled the requirements for the disbursement in advance can also apply for payment before the notes become due but at least one year after the notes' issuance (Mu 2011: 9). The application will be checked and evaluated through on-site examination and off-site surveillance at least 8 times. The ten evaluation items include the completeness of application materials for the payment, regulatory compliance and accountability of the reported investment and capital enlargement, regulatory compliance and accountability of CAR, compliance of NPLs' disposal, sound internal management system, significant progress in improving corporate governance, establishment of an information disclosure system, displacement of non-performing assets through special notes in accordance with laws, fulfillment of duties of provincial management agencies for RCCs in accordance with laws and realization of local supporting policies generally (Mu 2011: 11).

It is worth mentioning here that the CAR requirements are elevated in comparison to the original minimum levels set in the application plan for special notes' issuance: CAR for RCCs as separate entities at and under county level should be at least 2%, unified RCCs 4%, RCBs and RcoBs increase their CAR to 8% (Mu 2011: 276). If RCCs cannot fulfill the payment requirements within two years, the maturity can be extended to four or six years at most.

Once RCCs fulfill the requirements for the disbursement within the maturity of two years, the special notes can be cashed out as funds unquestionably owned by RCCs and the funds do not need to be paid back. NPLs and accumulative losses in the same value of funds from the special notes will be correspondingly removed from the balance sheet of RCCs.

According to the newest data, as of the end of 2010, 2408 counties and county-level cities have successfully applied for the issuance of special notes totaling RMB 169.9 (Mu 2011: 15). 97% of them (RMB 165 billion) were cashed by RCCs in 2366 counties and county-level cities (Mu 2011: 15). Altogether RMB 137.5 billion of the special notes were used to displace NPLs, and RMB 32.4 billion were used to offset accumulative losses (Mu 2011: 15).

Special lending is a kind of re-lending granted by the PBC with preferential lending rate of 0.945% (Mu 2011: 7). The loan rates are paid on a quarterly basis. The basic application unit of special lending is province. Special lending is offered also to offset NPLs and accumulative losses of insolvent RCCs. The conditionality of special lending is shown in that the issuance of special lending is separated into three stages. After the provincial government signs the contract with the China Development Bank, which represents the PBC to allocate special lending, the first 50% of special lending will be disbursed to the provincial government (Mu 2011: 11). When the average net capital of RCCs using special lending in this province increases by 50% from its value at the end of 2002, the provincial government can apply for the second round of disbursement of special lending, which will constitute 30% of the total amount. The remaining 20% will be distributed when the average net capital of all RCCs using special lending in this province is in the black. By the end of 2010, RMB 1.9 billion special lending was granted to RCCs in three provinces.

It should now be clear that the aim of the reformed funding policy is to release the historical burdens of large amount of NPLs and accumulative losses of RCCs, which were partly incurred because of political tasks carried out by RCCs. In this aspect, the funding policy has yielded good results. Between the end of 2002 and the end of 2010, NPLs decreased by RMB 196.5 billion and reached RMB 318.3 billion calculated in the old loan classification method (Mu 2011: 15). As of the end of 2010, the NPL ratio was only 5.6%, an abrupt reduction of 31% from the NPL ratio at the end of 2002 (Mu 2011: 15). Furthermore, the major part of the funding includes conditions requiring improvements in capital base, CAR, internal management system and corporate governance, as well as ownership transformation and management transfer to provincial government in participating RCCs. This public funding is also an effective incentive to encourage the reform process. In Zhengshe Mu's book about the reform of RCCs' corporate governance and management mechanism, Mr. Mu argues that the supporting policy is actually the price that was paid for the separation of RCCs from the central government. The State paid for the reform of RCCs and improved RCCs' assets' quality so that eventually provincial government would be more motivated to take over complete responsibility for RCCs' performance (Mu 2011: 44).

6.3   Features of new legal structures and transformation result

In contrast to the last round of reform, legal structures available to RCCs are not only limited to cooperative structures. For qualified RCCs in advanced localities with a high degree of urbanization, they can transform themselves into joint-stock banks or cooperative joint-stock banks. In densely populated localities or prefectures/municipalities/counties designated as grain or cotton production bases, RCCs and RCC unions are consolidated into a unified legal entity (Xie et al. 2005: 46). A last option is to keep the current two-tier system with RCCs and RCC unions as independent legal entities. The various financial organizations are RCBs, RcoBs, unified county RCCs and RCCs. The transformation requirements for RCCs into RCBs, RcoBs and unified county RCCs have already been given in the 15th document treated earlier. The main items like requirements for asset volume, minimum registered capital, CAR and NPL ratio are summarized in Table 6-4.

Table 6-4: Conditions for transformation into different types of financial institutions

RFIs	Asset volume	Minimum registered capital	CAR	NPLs' ratio	Founder number
RCBs	> RMB 1billion	RMB 50 million	≥8%	< 15%	≥500
RcoBs	n.a.	RMB 20 million	≥4%	<15%	≥1 000
Unified county RCCs	n.a.	RMB 10 million	≥4%	n.a.	≥1 000
Independent RCCs	n.a.	RMB 1 million	≥2%	n.a.	≥500

Source: Han 2009: 240; PBC 1997a

Note: at the end of 2006, the CBRC relaxed the conditions of entry for banking institutions in rural areas. The minimum registered capital for RcoBs was reduced from RMB 20 million to RMB 10 million and that for unified county RCCs was reduced from RMB 10 million to RMB 5 million (Xinhua News Agency 2009).

The aim of the transformation is to further promote the clarification of RCCs' property rights and to diversify rural financial institutions in China's countryside. Cooperatives shall no longer be the only formal financial institutions; more joint-stock and commercial banks should operate in rural areas. The type of structure RCCs choose for their restructuring depends on their own business situation.

In the last 10 years, the new freedom of rural financial institutions to exercise multiple property rights has been legislated in China. The result of the ownership transformation process is partially illustrated in Table 4-1 in chapter four. It shows only the change in the overall number of county level RCCs. Most county RCC unions chose to merge with township RCCs in their area to be one legal entity. The number of unified county RCCs increased from 94 in 2002 to 1976 in 2010 (see Table 4-1). There were only 132 county RCC unions left with separate independent legal status by the end of 2009. Many RCBs and RcoBs were built up through the merger of RCCs at and under the county or city level. 84% of all county level RCCs had been merged with township RCCs by the end of 2009. A nationwide merger of once dispersed and small RCCs is the first result of this reform. RCCs will be enlarged and enhanced through the unification. Risk resistance ability will also be augmented. Nevertheless, the unification also means a less competitive situation in the rural financial market.

In addition to the merger trend, this round of reform initiated commercialization of RCCs. By the end of 2010, 84 RCBs and 216 RcoBs had been set up. In recent year, the number of RCBs has been increasing steadily, and more and more qualified RcoBs have abandoned their cooperative nature in favor of becoming RCBs. The application for transformation into RCBs must be approved by the CBRC. Commercialization will make sure that RCCs can transform into real autonomous financial institutions responsible for their own profits and losses.

Having reviewed the organizational and systematic transformation of RCCs, the next question to be answered is the differences between these new legal structures and the former township and village RCCs. In the following section, special features of each new organizational form (e.g. shareholding structure, corporate governance and business orientation) will be described and analyzed according to relevant regulations. The aim of this introduction is to check the differences of former RCCs and new legal structures and to evaluate the advantages and disadvantages of this policy design.

6.3.1 Shareholder requirements and shareholding structure

Shareholder's regulation and shareholding structure requirements make up the most important part for the ownership transformation. The shareholder's regulation clearly defines shareholder groups and the shareholding structure requirements determine the concentration level and distribution situation of RCCs' equity shares.

The first organizational form to be introduced is RCB. RCBs are designed as pure joint-stock commercial banks. As one option for RCCs' transformation this is a new attempt. Requirements about RCBs' shareholding structure are regulated in the document "Interim provisions concerning management of rural commercial banks" published by the CBRC in 2003 (see Table 6-5). The group of RCBs' shareholders is defined as farmers, rural private businesses, rural enterprises and other economic organizations. From the strict requirements we can conclude that shareholding situation of RCBs is still dispersed. Legal person shareholders can hold a maximum 10% of total capital shares of RCBs. An absolute block-holder is prohibited. The regulation shows hesitation and cautiousness of the central government in the commercialization process. Controlling ownership by one or two legal person shareholders is undesirable. Furthermore, to protect RCCs from insider control, the employees' shares are limited to 25%.

Table 6-5: **Shareholding requirements for RCBs**

RFIs	Shareholding settings
RCBs	According to the "Interim provisions concerning management of rural commercial banks (2003)" RCBs should have at least 500 founders (CBRC 2003a). Shares issued by RCBs can be divided into natural person shares and legal person shares according to the nature of shareholders. Detailed requirements for RCBs' shareholding settings are like followings: 1. Each RCB share must be priced at RMB 1. 2. Every share has the same voting right. 3. Shares hold by a single natural person should not exceed 0.5% of total share capital. 4. Shares hold by a single legal person and its relative enterprises should not be above 10% of total share capital. 5. Employee shares of this RCB cannot be over 25% of total share capital. 6. Shares should be purchased in cash; the nominal value of the shares should be fully paid up at one time by the founders. 7. Founders of a RCB cannot exchange their shares three years after the RCB's establishment.

Source: CBRC 2003a

RcoBs can be seen as transitional organizational form somewhere between RCBs and RCCs. Though they are joint-stock banks, they also partially preserve the cooperative nature. Shares of RcoBs are not only divided into natural person shares and legal person shares but are also categorized into qualification shares and investment shares. Qualification shares are the fixed amount of shares which must be held by an RcoB's member. It is a kind of proof of membership in that particular RcoB. Investment shares, on the other hand, are extra shares purchased by RcoBs' members besides their qualification shares. This separation of shares gives small shareholders of qualification shares the possibility to hold shares in RcoBs and profit from the preferential services offered by the RcoBs, and wealthy investors have the possibility to hold more capital in RcoBs through the purchase of investment shares. Capital base of RcoBs is larger than original RCCs through the introduction of investment shares. The concentration level of shares can also be increased.

Table 6-6:   Shareholding requirements for RcoBs

RFIs	Shareholding settings
RcoBs	The regulation "Interim provisions concerning management of rural cooperative banks" was issued in 2003 by the CBRC. It has regulated in this document that RcoBs should have at least 1 000 founders and the registered capital should not be lower than RMB 20 million (CBRC 2003a). The CAR is regulated to reach 4% (CBRC 2003a). Important regulations about the shareholding structure of RcoBs are listed here: 1. Both qualification shares and investment shares are priced at RMB 1 for each. 2. RcoBs should set qualification shares amount for each shareholder according to their own situation. The minimal amount for natural person shareholders is RMB 1000 (this level can vary according to the regional conditions), for legal person shareholders the minimum amount is RMB 10 000. 3. Shareholders can make their own decisions about purchase amount of investment shares.

RFIs	Shareholding settings (Continuation)
RcoBs	4. Shareholders (members) of RcoBs enjoy priority to get access to RcoBs' services. Services provided for RcoBs' members are bounded with preferential conditions.
	5. Shareholders possessing investment shares can acquire dividends in accordance with the size of their investment shares.
	6. All members of RcoBs have one voting right based on their qualification shares. Natural person shareholders can get one more voting right when purchasing every 2 000 investment shares. Legal person shareholders on the other side have to purchase investment shares in size of 20 000 to getting one more voting right.
	7. Shares hold by a single natural person including single employee should not exceed 0.5% of total share capital.
	8. Total shares hold by this RcoB's employees should not be higher than 25% of total share capital.
	9. Shares hold by natural person shareholders excluding RcoBs' employees should not be less than 30% of total share capital.
	10. Shares hold by each legal person shareholder and its relative enterprises should not be higher than 10% of total share capital.
	11. Shares should be purchased in cash; the nominal value of the shares should be fully paid up at one time by the founders.
	12. Investment shares of RcoBs can be exchanged but cannot be withdrawn. After holding qualification shares for three years, shareholders can withdraw their qualification shares from RcoBs.

Source: CBRC 2003a

Unified county RCCs are still cooperative organizations. Since these RCCs have been merged together, financial risks they have to encounter increase. The capital requirements for them have to be increased at the same time. For this reason, unified county RCCs can increase the amount of obligation shares for membership and enlarge the shareholders' group.

Minimum natural person and legal person qualification share amount is regulated, but it should be implemented according to the real situation of unified county RCCs. Investment shares are similarly permitted. As a co-operative organization the percentage of natural person shareholders should not be lower than 50%, and the maximum shareholding level for legal person shareholders is only 5%. According to the regulation, the concentration level of shares in unified RCCs should be more dispersed than that of RCBs and RcoBs.

Table 6-7: **Shareholding requirements for unified county RCCs**

RFIs	**Shareholding settings**
Unified county RCCs	"Guidelines of the CBRC concerning the unification work of RCCs' legal person with county and city as basic unit" published by the CBRC in 2003 described the main principle, reasons and requirements for the unification of township RCCs with county and county-level city RCCs into one legal person. About construction of new ownership structure it's regulated that: 1. Increase the starting amount of shares in accordance with the regional economic situation and income level of farmers. 2. Enlarge shareholders' group: on the basis of existing members RCCs should integrate more farmers, individual industrial and commercial households, enterprises and other kinds of economic organizations into their shareholders' group. 3. Unified county RCCs can introduce "qualification shares" according to their own situation and add "investment shares" on the base of qualification shares.

RFIs	Shareholding settings (Continuation)
Unified county RCCs	4. Principally natural person shareholders and employees of RCCs have to buy at least RMB 1 000 qualification shares to get their membership. For legal person shareholders the level is set at RMB 10 000. The purchase amount of investment shares can be decided by shareholders themselves. 5. Shares hold by each natural person shareholder 6. should not be more than 0.5% of total share capital. 7. Total shares hold by RCCs' employees should not exceed 25% of total share capital. 8. Total shares hold by natural person shareholders excluding employees should not be less than 50% of total share capital. 9. Each legal person shareholder should not hold shares more than 5% of total share capital.

Source: CBRC 2003b

For independent RCCs, which didn't consolidate with county RCC unions, no special regulations were published about capital requirements and shareholding structure. I will cite here the "Administrative provisions on RCCs" published in 1997 by the PBC as reference, which is an important regulation for RCCs' management in the first round of reform in 1996.

Table 6-8: **Shareholding requirements for independent county/township/village RCCs**

RFIs	Shareholding settings
Independent county/ township/ village RCCs	It's regulated in this document that RCCs should have at least 500 members and the registered capital should not be less than RMB 1 million. The registered capital makes up of the paid equity capital from its members and the reserved capital. Requirements for shareholding structure are very simple: 1. Each member of RCC should not hold capital more than 2% of total share capital. 2. RCCs' shares can be exchanged after registered in the corresponding RCC. After the permission of the RCC's board of directors, shares can be withdrawn.

Source: PBC 1997a

Shareholding requirements about concentration level and maximum holding percentage of these RFIs mentioned above are summarized in Table 6-9. From this table, we can see that the shareholding structure of these RFIs is highly scattered. No controlling ownership is allowed. Moreover, RcoBs, unified county RCCs and other RCCs still organize their ownership structure around cooperative members and they service them with preferential conditions like other cooperative organizations as their main task. This conclusion is drawn from the required total natural person shares excluding employee shares of at least 30% for RcoBs and 50% for unified county RCCs and the constrained percentage of employee shares.

Table 6-9: **Requirements for shareholder structure of each type of RFIs**

RFIs/share type	Employee shares	Natural person shares	Legal person shares
RCBs	≤25%	Each ≤0.5%	Each ≤10%
RcoBs	≤25%	Each ≤0.5% total ≥30%	Each ≤10%
Unified county RCCs	≤25%	Each ≤0.5%, total ≥50%	Each ≤5%
Independent RCCs	n.a.	Each≤2%	Each≤2%

Another feature of these financial organizations is that RcoBs and unified county RCCs can also introduce investment shares, which can enrich their capital base on one side and further transform them from pure cooperative organizations into partly commercial ones. Moreover, in China the price for each share has also been regulated at RMB 1 per share both for qualification shares and for investment shares in all these RFIs. This pricing is possible, because these RFIs have not been listed in a stock market.

Last but not least, another common feature for all these cooperative organizations is that only natural persons, enterprises, private businesses and other types of economic organizations can hold shares at cooperative RFIs in their permanent registered residence (CBRC 2004f). Thus governments cannot become shareholders. Local governments can only donate capital to displace non-performing assets of cooperative RFIs (CBRC 2004f). The donated capital can be calculated as capital surplus, but cannot be counted as that government's shares (CBRC 2004f).

6.3.2 Corporate governance

To guarantee that owners can really own and manage their belonging agent here RCCs, a sound corporate governance structure has to be established. We will first look at the historical development of corporate governance of RCCs. RCCs' corporate governance with cooperative patterns had already been restored during the RCC reform between 1982 and 1984. A measure that was taken to resume the cooperative nature back to RCCs was to restore the members' representative meeting. According to the original idea, managers of RCCs should be elected by the members of

RCCs. This is the simple form of cooperative corporate governance of RCCs. Because RCCs operated at that time under the directives of the ABC, the members' representative meeting did not really come into play. After the separation of RCCs from the ABC in 1996, a real corporate governance structure was set up (see Figure 6-2). The concrete requirements for the corporate governance structure is regulated in the "Administrative provisions on RCCs" published by the PBC in 1997.

Figure 6-2:   **Corporate governance structure of a cooperative organization**

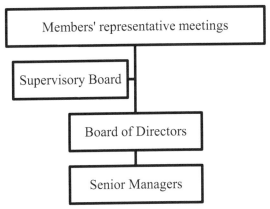

Source: PBC 1997a

Figure 6-2 shows the general corporate governance structure of a cooperative organization. The highest governing body of a cooperative organization is the members' representative meeting. In RCCs each member has only one vote. Members can choose their favorite representatives with their one vote to attend the members' representative meeting. Through the members' representative meeting, the interests of members should be spoken up and members can be integrated into the decision-making process for big issues. Furthermore, members have the right to elect and change members of the board of directors, who should represent them to deal with business of RCCs. The supervisory board's members are also elected in the members' representative meetings. The supervisory board plays an intern supervisory role over the board of directors and checks the regulation compliance of RCCs' business. The decisions of the board of directors are exercised by senior managers of a cooperative organization under the leadership of the board of directors.

The description above shows the working method of this corporate governance and the tasks of each governance body. From the aspect of principal agent theory, four principal-agent relationships can be identified in this governance structure from the first sight: namely, between members and members' representatives meeting; between members' representative meeting and the board of directors; between members' representative meeting and the supervisory board; and between the board of directors and the senior managers (see Table 6-10).

Moreover, the "Administrative provisions on RCCs" (1997) has regulated that president and vice-president of the board of directors should be nominated by county RCC unions and the qualification of them should be investigated by the county branch of the PBC and then the board of the directors can vote for its president and vice president (PBC 1997a). Senior managers of RCCs should be chosen in the same way (PBC 1997a). This means, two new principal-agent relationships should be added into the whole principal-agency-complex (see Table 6-10). The first is between county RCC union and president and vice president of the board of directors, and the other between county RCC union and senior manager of RCC. Here is to mention that before 2003 the county RCC unions and township and village RCCs did not merge together and were different legal entities. County RCC unions should only serve the participating RCCs and coordinate their business. This multiple-principal-agent relationship can make the whole structure vulnerable to moral hazard and interest conflicts between principals and agents.

Table 6-10: Multiple-principal-agent relationships in RCCs from 1996 to 2003

Principals	Agents
Members	Members' representative meeting
Members' representative meeting	Board of Directors
Members' representative meeting	Supervisory Board
Board of Directors	Senior managers
County RCC union	President & vice president of Board of Directors
County RCC union	Senior manager of RCC

So the board of directors has two principals, namely the members' representative meeting and county RCC union. Senior manager of RCCs also has two principals the board of directors and county RCC union. County RCC unions were established to be responsible for the management of RCCs in their regions and represent interests of governments. Their nomination right for most important positions in their subordinate RCCs makes them the real principal of all governance bodies in RCCs. The whole modern corporate governance structure cannot really come into play because of the nomination clause.

During the RCC reform in 2003, this basic organizational structure of corporate governance used by RCCs since 1996 was taken over by RCBs, RcoBs and unified county RCCs, but a lot of improvements have been made in the regulation. The main functioning bodies of them are the general shareholders' meeting, the board of directors, the supervisory board and senior managers. Here the general shareholders' meeting has replaced the members' representative meeting as the highest decision-making organ. President of the board of directors is the legal representative of the corresponding RFIs.

Important improvements are listed below:

First of all, independent directors were introduced for the first time in the board of directors in RCBs and RcoBs. Independent directors should represent the interests of depositors, middle and small shareholders.

Secondly, the compositions of the board of directors and the supervisory board of RCBs and RcoBs are defined clearly and in great detail. The

151

"Administrative provisions on RCCs" of 1997 only regulated that members of the board of directors should come from the membership of RCCs. Members of the supervisory board should make up of members' representatives and staff representatives. The "Interim provisions concerning management of rural commercial banks" regulated, however, that the board of directors should have between 7 and 19 members. Employees should constitute at least 1/4 and at the most 1/3 of total board members (see Table 6-11). Natural person shareholders except employee shareholders should hold at least 1/4 seats in the board of directors. About the supervisory board of RCBs, it's regulated that there should be between 5 and 9 members in the supervisory board. At most 1/3 of them should be staff representatives, elected by the RCB's employees. The non-employee members of the supervisory board should be elected by the shareholders' meeting.

Table 6-11: **Composition of the board of directors and the supervisory board of RCBs, RcoBs and unified county RCCs**

RFIs	Board of directors	Supervisory board
Members' number	7 – 19 members (for RCBs and RcoBs)	5 – 9 members (for RCBs and RcoBs)
RCBs	$1/3 \geq$ Employees$\geq 1/4$ Natural person shareholders except employees $\geq 1/4$	$1/3 \geq$ Employees
RcoBs	$1/3 \geq$ Employees Representatives of rural households and rural private businesses $\geq 1/3$	$1/3 \geq$ Employees
Unified county RCCs	$1/3 \geq$ Employees Natural person shareholders except employees $\geq 1/2$	Non-employee members $\geq$ 1/3

Source: CBRC 2003a / CBRC 2003b

We can see from the regulation that the number of employees in the board of directors and the supervisory board is strictly confined to a maximum of 1/3 so that the board of directors will not be heavily controlled by insiders. The proportion of natural person shareholders is also required to be above 1/4 in RCBs and above 1/3 in RcoBs. This ensures that the interests of normal natural person shareholders are protected.

Thirdly, nomination authority of the upper-levels of RCC unions for important positions in RFIs is not mentioned in regulations for all the newly restructured entities.

A scientific and democratic regulatory framework has been built up with the publication of corresponding regulations in China; next job is the implementation. Important factors for a fluid implementation include shareholders' awareness of their rights and responsibilities, information transparency between insiders and shareholders and qualified members in the supervisory board and the board of directors. Effective decision-making mechanism, execution mechanism and supervision mechanism should be set up. Sound corporate governance is an indispensable requirement for a sustainable development of rural financial organizations.

6.3.3 Tai'an Case study of the institutional transformation

The case chosen here is Tai'an city in Shandong Province (see Figure 6-3). Shandong Province is one of the first eight provinces and municipalities that took part in the reform in 2003. Data used here sources from the journal article "An empirical study of property rights' reform of Rural Credit Cooperatives in Shandong Province" of Lei Song and Jiachuan Wang. This empirical report shows the change of RCCs in Tai'an city in the apect of their capital volume, gradual change of shareholding strucutre and evaluation of RCCs' corporate governance through questionnaires. From the data introduced here we can get a first impression about the reform results.

Figure 6-3:   Location of Shandong Province on the map of China

Source: http://daxueyingyu.com/places-in-china/

During the reform in 2003, counties in Tai'an merge their grassroots RCCs into one legal entity. According to the newest data on the website of provincial RCC union of Shandong Province, there are now a unified RCC in **Taishan district** of Tai'an city, a unified RCC in **Daiyue district** of Tai'an city, a unified county RCC of **Feicheng county-level city**, a unified county RCC of **Xintai county-level city**, a unified county RCC of **Ningyang county** and a RcoB in **Dongping county** (http://www.sdnxs. com/Channel/39171). From the real example, we can see that former dispersed RCCs merge together either at the district level or at county level into six large-scaled RCC unions. Most of them chose the organizational form of unified county RCCs, only Dongping county selected the form of RcoBs.

The overall shareholding situation of all RCCs in Tai'an city from 2002 to 2005 was summerized in the journal article of Lei Song and Jiachuan Wang mentioned above. The data is very detailed and can give a very clear picture of overall share distribution of all RCCs in this city. Since RCCs in Tai'an city have transformed either to unified county RCCs or RcoBs. Their shares were accordingly divided into qualification shares and investment shares. From 2002 to 2005 net capital of RCCs in Tai'an city increased from RMB 482.78 million to RMB 1.15 billion, which is a 1.4-fold increase. From the perspective of shareholding structure, the

154

percentage of RCCs' qualifacation shares decreased steadily from 94.28% at the end of 2002 to 42.22% at the end of 2005, while the percentage of investment shares increased from 5.72% at the end of 2002 to 57.78% at the end of 2005 (see Table 6-12). When we take the increase of capital volume in consideration, the real amount of qualification shares did not change much. The main increase of capital should be ascribed to the increase of investment shares.

Table 6-12: **Proportion change of qualification shares and investment shares from 2002 to 2005 in Tai'an city**

Share Types	End of 2002	End of 2003	End of 2004	End of 2005
Qualification shares	94.28%	92.51%	42.92%	42.22%
Investment shares	5.72%	7.49%	57.08%	57.78%

Source: Song / Wang 2007: 71

In the same period, natural person shares sank slightly from 95.35% at the end of 2002 to 83.13% at the end of 2005 (see Table 6-13). In contrast to the slight decrease of nature person shares we see a significant fall of farmers' shares from 92.04% at the end of 2002 to 63.57% at the end of 2005. Percentage of qualification shares of farmers sunk from 92.03% in 2002 to 40.53% in 2005. We can drive some conclusion from the change of available data: Farmers were the biggest contributors to the qualification shares. Along with the capital replenishment, more and more employees, enterprises and other organizations engage in the purchase of investment shares of RCCs. Farmers also invested their money to purchase investment shares in RCCs, which can be shown by the increase of farmers' investment shares from 0.01% in 2002 to 23.04% in 2005.

Table 6-13: Proportion change of natural person shares and legal person shares from 2002 to 2005 in Tai'an city

Share types	Shareholders	End of 2002	End of 2003	End of 2004	End of 2005
Natural person shares	Sum	95.35%	93.26%	91.45%	83.13%
	Farmers' shares	92.04% Q:92.03% I: 0.01%	92.49% Q:92.49% I: 0	82.58% Q:41.33% I: 41.25%	63.57% Q:40.53% I: 23.04%
	Employee shares	3.31% Q: 0 I: 3.31%	0.77% Q: 0 I: 0.77%	8.87% Q: 0.7% I: 8.17%	19.56% Q: 0.8% I: 18.76%
Legal person shares	Sum	4.65% Q: 2.25% I: 2.40%	6.74% Q: 0.02% I: 6.72%	8.55% Q: 0.89% I: 7.66%	16.87% Q: 0.89% I: 15.98%

Source: Song / Wang 2007: 71

Note: "Q" represents qualification shares; "I" represents investment shares.

Here is to mention that the period between 2002 and 2005 is the beginning phase of the reform. The shareholding structure shows clear tendency towards decrease of farmers' percentage and increase of percentage of investment shares.

Besides the changes of shareholding structure, questionnaires have investigated the situation of corporate governance in Tai'an city. The results were concluded from 400 questionnaires made in over 120 grassroots RCCs in Tai'an city. 80.7% of effective questionnaires confirmed the improvement of effectiveness of the general shareholders' meeting, the board of directors and the supervisory board in contrast to the situation before the restructuring. This is the first good sign. The second question is about the generation method of presidents of the board of directors and supervisors and senior managers of RCCs (see Table 6-14).

Table 6-14: Questionnaire results about the generation way of important positions of RCCs in Tai'an

Positions	Elected by the board	Appointed by the upper-level authority	No idea
President of the board of directors	27.9%	69.7%	2.4%
President of the supervisory board	35.7%	62.4%	1.9%
Senior managers of RCCs	57.3% hired by the board of directors	42.7%	0

Source: Song / Wang 2007:72

The result of this question is not so positive. 69.7% of the effective questionnaires thought president of the board of directors was appointed by the upper-level authority. 62.4% of them agreed that president of the supervisory board was delegated by the upper-level authority. Here the sign of administrative management is still patent.

6.4 Provincial RCC unions as management authorities

The management transfer from the central government to the provincial government is both as positive and as negative assessed by Chinese researchers. Originally RCCs were centrally established by the Chinese government and the management right over all RCCs was in the hands of central government. After collectivization movement in 1959, the management right was transferred downward to the local production brigades or village cadres. Since 1979, RCCs were subordinated to the centrally owned bank ABC. In the first round of reform in 1996, the PBC retook its management right over RCCs and fulfilled at the same time the supervision tasks. Criticized was the PBC for its double role both as a manager and a referee. In this round of reform in 2003, it has clearly regulated that the central government and the central bank of China should give their management right over RCCs to the provincial government. Tasks of the provincial government can be found in the 15th document in chapter 6.1.2.

Provincial RCC unions were established to fulfill the management and regulatory work. The regulatory reference for the establishment of provincial RCC unions is the "Interim provisions concerning management of RCC unions in provinces (autonomous regions and municipalities directly under the central government)" published by the CBRC in 2003. According to the regulation all county or county-level RCCs and RcoBs in one province can purchase shares in the corresponding provincial RCC union voluntarily. RCBs can also involve in provincial RCC union according to their own wishes (CBRC 2003c). But in reality RCBs are obligated to join the provincial RCC union. The tasks of provincial RCC unions include management, guidance, coordination and offering services to subordinated RCCs. Provincial RCC unions cannot engage into public financial services like taking deposits from the public and offering loan services to the public.

Positive argument is that this management transfer is not like before. Losses of RCCs will not be bailed out by the central government any more. The ultimate management right of RCCs is in the hands of provincial government. It's said that the special notes granted by the central bank is the price paid by the central government for provincial governments to take over RCCs. This sinking of management authority has the advantage that RCCs can be managed with concern of regional specificities. The policies designed for them are more specific and targeted. Furthermore, a settlement system at the provincial level is possible through the unified management in a province. Another positive effect of this management transfer is that the supervision and management of RCCs is separately executed by two different authorities. The CBRC at the provincial level takes the responsibility of supervision. This separation guarantees a better oversee of RCCs' work.

Negative observed is the risk disposal responsibility of provincial government for RCCs in its administrative area. The system uses administrative management to replace regulation. As we all know, regulators bear no risk while the manager has no one to blame. Provincial government as final managers of RCCs has to pay for their losses. This policy regulation is against the principle of the reform that RCCs should be transformed into real autonomous, disciplined market players responsible for their own losses and developments. Since this responsibility is not equal to the regulated rights enjoyed by provincial government, provincial government will try to intervene into the business of RCCs so that risks of RCCs will be avoided. This risk-avoiding tendency sometimes does not coincide with the interests of RCCs. The result is that it's a common phenomenon that provincial government appoints senior managers for RCCs.

Moreover all RCCs have to become members of the provincial RCC management authority which constitutes a de facto monopoly and precludes any outside competition (Xie et al 2005:35).

The organization for the RCCs management at the provincial level is different. According to the "Interim provisions concerning management of RCC unions in provinces (autonomous regions and municipalities directly under the central government" the provincial government can decide in what way RCCs should be administered (CBRC 2003c). They can set up a provincial union of RCCs or any other organization to take up the job if they find it appropriate. No restrictions are imposed on their choice (Cheng: 10).

Now in China, except in Beijing, Shanghai and Tianjing where RCCs are reorganizing themselves into a rural commercial bank or a rural cooperative bank; in other pilot provinces have a provincial RCC union was set up in each province as a legal entity, which is controlled jointly by county RCCs.

6.5   Result and evaluation of RCC reform in 2003

The first direct result of this round of RCC reform is that RCCs are no longer dispersed grassroots RFIs. Through this reform method most of RCCs chose to merge into county RCCs. Furthermore, new organizational forms were introduced to be the alternatives for the transformation of RCCs. RCCs can according to their own business situation transform into RCBs or RcoBs. Moreover, the performance and overall business situation of RCCs get improved in the last 10 years. A summary of the data in 2002 and 2010 was made to illustrate the changes (see Table 6-15).

Table 6-15: Comparison of main balance sheet items of rural cooperative financial institutions in 2002 and 2010

Unit: RMB billion and %

Items/Year	2002	2010
Assets	n.a. but 2689.4 in 2003	10658.3
Outstanding deposits	1987.4	8,800.0
Outstanding loans	1393.7	5900.0
NPLs	514.7	318.3
NPL ratio	36.93	5.6
CAR	-8.5%	n.a.
Net profit	-5.8	67.8

Source: data in Table 4-3/CBRC 2007b: 133

Note: NPL, NPL ratio and CAR are calculated using the old loan classification method.

Among the three kinds of organizational forms, both RcoBs and RCBs show high profit-making ability (see Table 6-16). ROA level of RCBs and RcoB has reached the average ROA of all banking institutions in China in 2011 (see Table 2-21). But the high ROE and ROA cannot indicate that these organizational forms are better and more suitable organizational forms than RCCs, because at the beginning the establishment require-ments for RcoBs and RCBs were higher than that of RCCs.

Table 6-16: ROE and ROA of rural cooperative financial institutions from 2007 to 2011

Unit: %

RFIs/Year	Items	2007	2008	2009	2010	2011
RCCs	ROA	0.45	0.42	0.41	0.36	0.74
	ROE	10.36	9.87	9.72	8.34	15.30
RCBs	ROA	0.70	0.79	0.80	1.01	1.20
	ROE	12.97	13.71	13.36	13.82	15.43
RcoBs	ROA	0.84	1.03	1.05	1.19	1.30
	ROE	13.29	15.87	15.85	16.05	17.06

Source: PBC 2013d: 3

The lending business of these RFIs to rural households did not change a lot (see Figure 2-5 in chapter 2). In 2002 66.44 billion rural households acquired loans from rural cooperative financial institution (PBC 2011: 70).

The number of rural households increased to 82.42 billion in 2009, 33.5% of total number of rural households (see Table 6-17). This development does not match with the quick increase of these RFIs' business scale, though, the amount of loans granted to rural households by rural cooperative financial institutions increased from RMB 1165.492 billion in 2007 to RMB 2700 billion in 2012 (see Table 2-10 in chapter 2).

Table 6-17: **Number and proportion of rural households getting loans from rural cooperative financial institutions from 2002 to 2009**

Unit: billion and %

Year/Number and proportion of rural households	Number of rural households	Proportion of the total number of rural households
2002	66.44	29.68
2003	77.16	33.82
2004	79.90	35.63
2005	83.70	36.19
2006	86.52	37.19
2007	78.17	33.20
2008	77.83	32.04
2009	77.83	33.50

Source: PBC 2011: 70

Overall speaking, although the coverage ratio of rual cooperative financial institutions among rural households did not increase much during the last 10 years, the overall situation of rural cooperative financial institutions has improved itself a lot. The reform can be seen as success from the perspective of the realization of reform aims. As I have illustrated through the case study in Tai'an city, the ownership of these rural cooperative financial institutions has be clarified and the capital base of these was enlarged. Furthermore, new forms of organization were also established according to the requirements of corporate governance and shareholding structure. The only concern is that according to the survey the senior managers of RCCs are still partly appointed by the upper-level authority. This is against the basic requirement of modern corporate governance, according to which the rights of shareholders should be placed at the first place.

7. Conclusion and prospect for the further development

Through analysis we can conclude that the cooperative financial institutions didnot achieve success and have hardly realized the cooperative concept in the last 60 years. The most important reason for that is the cooperative idea for financial institutions, which came originally from Germany, was introduced in China as a policy tool from top to down. A social foundation for cooperative financial institutions was not available in China and the cooperative concept was not really accepted by rural citizens. This given defect determined development difficulties of RCCs. Like other policy instruments, which didnot take the social background into consideration, RCCs cannot achieve sustainable development and have to be reformed.

RCC reform is only one part of the privatization and commercializaton of rural financial market in China. Through the last 10 year reform experiences, RCCs have successfully transformed to market-oriented and private-owned rural financial institutions. The reform of RCCs does not stop here. The CBRC published "Guiding opinions of the CBRC on accelerating the shareholding transformation of rural cooperative financial institutions" in 2010 and set the goal of realizing a shareholding reform of all rural cooperative financial institutions within the next five years (CBRC 2010d). Qualification shares would be abandoned (CBRC 2010d). To formulate the goal in another way, according to the plan of the CBRC, in the next five years all RCCs and RcoBs will be transformed to RCBs.

For the existing RCBs, their commercialization also goes further. In December 2010 the first RCB, Chongqing RCB, went public on the Hong Kong Stock Exchange. It raised US$1.48 billion in an IPO in Hong Kong (Soh / Thomas 2010). The four RCBs of Zhangjiagang, Wujiang, Changshu and Jiangyin in Jiangsu Province have received approval for an IPO (Subrahmanyam 2011). The CBRC also issued accordingly the regulation "Consolidation paper on listing requirements for RCBs" and set the minimum asset base for RCBs to be listed should be RMB 70 billion.

From all these trials we see the determination of the central government to privatize RCCs. Questioned is whether commercial oriented RCBs can really better serve the financial needs in the Chinese rural areas and how the poor can also get financial support from these profit-oriented financial institutions, especially in the background that rural cooperative financial institutions still make up the dominant part in terms of financial supply in the Chinese rural financial market. These questions will be subjects for the further research.

Bibliography

- (unknown): 中国农村信用社的改革和发展 *Reform and development of RCCs in China*, available: http://www.afdc.org.cn/afdc/UploadFile/200931848851549.ppt [16.3.2013].

- (unknown): *PRC regulation and supervision*, available: http://www.hkexnews.hk/ reports/prelist/Documents/E110_2.pdf[18.9.2012].

- (2005): 良好邮政储蓄改革：牵一发动全身 *Good postal savings reform: a slight move in one part may affect the whole situation*, available: http://finance.sina. com.cn/ money/bank/bank_yhpl/20050906/11481945326.shtml [7. 5. 2012].

- (2006): 小额信贷公司的山西实验 *The experiment of microfinance lending companies in Shanxi Province*, available: http://www.cnhubei.com/200611/ca12 12791.htm [16.5.2012].

- (2007): 组建统一法人后农村信用社信贷风险产生原因及化解 *The cause and solution of credit risks emerged after set-up of RCCs with unified legal person status*, available: http://www.wenmi114.com/wenmi/lunwen/jingjilunwen/2007-07-26/20070726109142.html[10.3.2012].

- (2007): 统一法人改革后县（市）农村信用联社经营问题研究 *Study on the management problems of Rural Credit Unions in countis and cities after the unification of the legal person*, available: http://www.zgjrjw.com/news/ncjrgz/ 2007922/11222 668872.html[15.3.2012].

- (2011a): *The transformation of RCCs into commercial banks will be finished in the next 5 years*, available: http://www.cfi.net.cn/p20110803000140.html[16.12.2011].

- (2011b): 中国银监会将实施新的审慎监管框架 *The CBRC will implement new supervisory framework*, available:http://www.caijing.com.cn/2011-02-22/110647106 .html [21.6.2012].

- (2011c): 巴塞尔协议III与"十二五"中国银行业监管新框架 *The Basel III and new supervisory framework of Chinese banking sector during the 12th five-year-plan*, available: http://money.163.com/11/0217/11/6T3E0IJ40025335.html[5.10.2012].

- (2012): 农信社产权制度选择不宜一刀切 *Not using "one size fits all" principle when selecting ownership system for RCCs*, available: http://www.nongxinyin.com/pay/ html/FF2D60103E334BB897253C0D0A7E570D.htm[13.7.2013].

ABC (2005): *ABC annual report 2004*, available: http://www.abchina.com/en/about-us/annual-report/2004/[20.12.2012].

ABC (2006): *ABC annual report 2005*, available: http://www.abchina.com/en/about-us/annual-report/2005/[20.12.2012].

ABC (2007): *ABC annual report 2006,* available: http://www.abchina.com/en/about-us/annual-report/2006/[20.12.2012].

ABC (2008): *ABC annual report 2007*, available: http://www.abchina.com/en/about-us/annual-report/2007/[20.12.2012].

ABC (2009): *ABC annual report 2008*, available: http://www.abchina.com/en/about-us/annual-report/2008/[20.12.2012].

ABC (2010): *ABC annual report 2009*, available: http://www.abchina.com/en/about-us/annual-report/2009/[20.12.2012].

ABC (2011): *ABC annual report 2010*, available: http://www.abchina.com/en/about-us/annual-report/2010/[20.12.2012].

ABC (2012a): *ABC annual report 2011*, available: http://www.abchina.com/en/ about us/annual-report/2011/[20.12.2012].

ABC (2012b): *ABC corporate social responsibility report 2011*, available: http://www.abchina.com/CN/AboutABC/CSR/CSRReport/201203/t20120323_216624.h tm[21.8.2013].

ABC (2013a): *ABC corporate social responsibility report 2012*, available: http://www.abchina.com/cn/AboutABC/Csr/CSRReport/201303/t20130326_326088.htm [21.8.2013].

ABC (2013b): *ABC annual report 2012*, available: http://www.abchina.com/ en/about-us/annual-report/2012/[25.8.2013].

ABC / PBC (1987): 关于农村信用社信贷资金管理的暂行规定 *Interim provisions about RCCs' credit asset* management, available: http://www.chinalawedu.com/ news/1200/22016/22021/22178/2006/3/yi323193040112360027332-0.htm[5.8.201 2].

Adams, D. W. / Graham, D. H./Von Pischke, J. D. (1984): *Undermining rural development with cheap credit*, Boulder CO: Westview Press.

ADB (1997): *Technical assistance to the People's Republic of China for the reform of the Rural Credit Cooperative system*, Manila: ADB.

ADBC (2005a): *Brief history of the ADBC*, available: http://www.adbc.com.cn/temp lates/T_secondEN/index.aspx?nodeid=87&page=ContentPage&contentid=5937[30.12.2 011].

ADBC (2005b): *Sources of funds and its uses of the ADBC*, available: http://www. adbc.com.cn/templates/T_secondEN/index.aspx?nodeid=87&page=ContentPage&conte ntid=5938[30.12.2011].

ADBC (2005c): *Business scope of the ADBC*, available: http://www.adbc.com.cn/temp lates/T_secondEN/index.aspx?nodeid=87&page=ContentPage&contentid=5939[30.12.2 011].

ADBC (2005d): *Organizational structure of the ADBC*, available: http://www.adbc. com.cn/templates/T_secondEN/index.aspx?nodeid=88[30.12.2011].

ADBC (2011): *ADBC annual report 2010*, available: http://www.adbc.com.cn/ re-port/2010report/en/1.htm[1.1.2012].

ADBC (2012): *ADBC annual report 2011*, available: http://www.adbc.com.cn/ re-port/2011report/en/1.htm[23.8.2013].

ADBC (2013): *ADBC Annual report 2012*, available: http://www.adbc.com.cn/report/ 2012report/en/0.htm[23.8.2013].

Aglietta, M. / Rebérioux, A. (2005): *Corporate governance adrift*, Cheltenham & North-ampton: Edward Elgar Publishing Limited.

166

Arun, T. G. / Turner, J. (2009): "Corporate governance of banks in developing economies: concepts and issues", in: Arun / Turner (ed.), *Corporate governance and development - reform, financial systems and legal frameworks*, Cheltenham & Northampton: Edward Elgar Publishing Limited.

Bai, C. (2010): "Chinese microfinance networks and cooperation patters", in: World Microfinance Forum Geneva (ed.), *Microfinance in China*, available: http://www. microfinanceforum.org/wp-content/uploads/2012/03/ChinaCompendium-eVersion.pdf[20.8.2013].

BCBS (1988): *International convergence of capital measurement and capital standards*, available: http://www.bis.org/publ/bcbsc111.htm[9.9.2013].

BCBS (1992): *A framework for measuring and managing liquidity*, available: http://www.bis.org/publ/bcbs10b.htm[20.11.2012].

BCBS (2000): *Sound practices for managing liquidity in banking organizations*, available: http://www.bis.org/publ/bcbs69.htm[23.10.2012].

BCBS (2004): *International convergence of capital measurement and capital standards (a revised framework)*, available: http://www.bis.org/publ/bcbs107.htm[17. 9.2012].

BCBS (2006): *Basel II: International convergence of capital measurement and capital standards: a revised framework - comprehensive version*, available: http://www.bis. org/publ/bcbs128.htm[9.9.2013].

BCBS (2008): *Liquidity risk: management and supervisory challenges*, available: http://www.bis.org/publ/bcbs136.htm[20.11.2012].

BCBS (2008): *Principles for sound liquidity risk management and supervision - final document*, available: http://www.bis.org/publ/bcbs144.htm[20.11.2012].

BCBS (2010): *Basel III: International framework for liquidity risk measurement, standards and* monitoring, available: http://www.bis.org/publ/bcbs188.pdf [5.10.2012].

BCBS (2011): Basel III: *A global regulatory framework for more resilient banks and banking systems - revised version June 2011, available*: http://www.bis.org/publ/bcbs189.htm[9.9.2013].

Bell, S. K. / Chao, H. (2010): *The financial system in China - risks and opportunities following the global financial crisis*, available: http://www.pacificpension.org/ upload/China's%20Financial%20System%20-%20Howard%20Chao.pdf[25.11.2012].

Berger, A. N. / Herring, R. J. / Szegö, G. P. (1995): *The role of capital in financial institutions*, available: http://fic.wharton.upenn.edu/fic/papers/95/9501.pdf[11.7. 2013].

Bureau of Statistics of Jiangsu Province (2011): *The statistical year book of Jiangsu province of 2011*, available: http://www.jssb.gov.cn/2011nj/nj01/nj01001.htm [14.4.2012].

Cai, E. (1999): "Financial supervision in China: framework, methods and current issues", in: BIS (ed.), *Policy papers No. 7 - strengthening the banking system in China: issues and experience*, available: http://www.bis.org/publ/plcy07k.pdf [26.5.2012].

Cai, F. (2010a): 蔡昉文选 *Analects of Caifang*, Beijing: China Modern Economic Publishing House.

Cai, F. (2010b): *Transforming the Chinese economy*, available: http://books.google.co m.hk/books?id=hKTmJyPRwZgC&printsec=frontcover&hl=zh-TW#v=onepage&q &f=false[14.5.2013].

CBRC (unknown): *The reforms of rural credit cooperatives have achieved significant progress*, available: http://www.cbrc.gov.cn/EngdocView.do?docID=1494 [7.5.2013].

CBRC (2003a): 关于"农村商业银行管理暂行规定"和"农村合作银行管理暂行规定"的通知 *Notice of the CBRC on issuing "Interim provisions concerning management of Rural Commercial Banks" and "Interim provisions concerning management of Rural Cooperative Banks"*, available：http://www.cbrc.gov.cn/chinese/ home/ docDOC_Read View/283.html[1.1.2012].

CBRC (2003b):关于农村信用社以县（市）为单位统一法人的指导意见 *Guidelines of the CBRC concerning the unification work of RCCs' legal person with county and city as basic unit)*, available: http://www.cbrc.gov.cn/chinese/home/doc DOC_ReadView/285.html[1.1.2012].

CBRC (2003c): 关于印发"农村信用社省（自治区，直辖市）联合社管理暂行规定的通知" *Notice of the CBRC on issuing "interim provisions concerning management of RCC unions in provinces (autonomous regions and municipalities directly under the Central Government"*, available: http://www.cbrc.gov.cn/chinese/ home/docDOC_ReadView/287.html[1.1.2012].

CBRC (2003d): 中华人民共和国银行监督管理法 *Order of the President of the People's Republic of China; Law of the People's Republic of China on banking regulation and supervision*, available: http://www.cbrc.gov.cn/EngdocView.do?docID= 554[4.6.2012].

CBRC (2004a): 农村合作金融机构风险评价和预警指标体系（试行）*Provisional risk assessment and risk forewarning index system for rural cooperative financial institutions*, available: http://blog.csdn.net/yuanfen127/article/details/2025472 [27. 6.2012].

CBRC (2004b): 股份制商业银行风险评级体系（暂行）*Provisional risk assessment system for joint-stock commercial banks*, *available*: www.cbrc.gov.cn/chinese/home/docDOC_ReadView/301.html[1.1.2012].

CBRC (2004c): 商业银行资本充足率管理办法 *Regulation governing capital adequacy of commercial banks*, available: http://www.cbrc.gov.cn/EngdocView.do?doc ID=558 [11.7.2012].

CBRC (2004d): 商业银行不良资产监测和考核暂行办法 *Provisional rules monitoring and assessment of non-performing assets of commercial banks*, available: http://www.cbrc.gov.cn/chinese/home/docDOC_ReadView/309.html[25.11.2012].

CBRC (2004e): 商业银行与内部人和股东关联交易管理办法 *Administrative rules governing the connected lending between commercial banks and their insiders/ shareholders*, available: www.cbrc.gov.cn/upload/zwgk/ml3/2/5-1-5.doc [10.12.2012].

CBRC (2004f): 关于规范向农村合作金融机构入股的若干意见 *Several opinions of the CBRC on regulating purchase of shares of rural cooperative financial institutions*, *a*vailable: http://wenku.baidu.com/view/38f6022f3169a4517723a3a8.html [17.5.2013].

CBRC (2005a): 商业银行内部控制评价试行办法 *Provisional rules on internal control assessment of commercial banks*, available: www.cbrc.gov.cn/chinese/home/docDOC_ReadView/1121.html[18.6.2012].

CBRC (2005b): 商业银行市场风险管理指引 *Guidelines on market risk management of commercial banks*, available: www.cbrc.gov.cn/chinese/home/docDOC_Read View/1123.html[18.6.2012].

CBRC (2005c): *NPLs of major commercial banks as of Dec. 31, 2004,* available: http://www.cbrc.gov.cn/EngdocView.do?docID=1154[18.12.2012].

CBRC (2005d): *商业银行风险监管核心指标（试行）Core indicators for risk-based supervision of commercial banks (Tentative),* available: http://www.cbrc.gov.cn/chinese/home/ docDOC_ReadView/2196.html[18.6.2012].

CBRC (2006a): *关于进一步做好农村合作金融机构贷款风险分类工作的通知 Notice of the CBRC on further strengthening risk-based loan classification work at rural cooperative financial institutions,* available: http://www.cbrc.gov.cn/chinese/ home/doc Doc_ReadView/2565.html[1.1.2012].

CBRC (2006b): *关于印发农村合作金融机构社团贷款指引的通知 Notice of the CBRC on issuing group credit by rural cooperative financial institutions,* available: http://www.cbrc.gov.cn/chinese/home/docDOC_ReadView/2541.html[1.1.2012].

CBRC (2006c): *商业银行合规风险管理指引 Regulation on compliance risk management of commercial banks,* available: www.cbrc.gov.cn/chinese/home/ docDOC_ReadView/ 2835.html[18.6.2012].

CBRC (2006d): *银行业金融机构信息系统风险管理指引 Regulation on management of information system risk of banking financial institutions,* available: www.cbrc .gov.cn/chinese/home/docDOC_ReadView/2840.html[18.6.2012].

CBRC (2006e): *NPLs of commercial banks in 2005,* available: http://www.cbrc.gov. cn/EngdocView.do?docID=1392[18.12.2012].

CBRC (2006f): *Notable achievements registered in the reform of RCCs,* available: http://www.cbrc.gov.cn/EngdocView.do?docID=2299[3.6.2013].

CBRC (2006g): *中国银行监督管理委员会关于印发《农村合作金融机构信贷资产风险分类指引》的通知 Notice of the CBRC on issuing "Guidelines on risk-based loan classification in rural cooperative financial institutions",* available: http://www.cbrc.gov .cn/upload/zwgk/ml3/2/5-2-10.doc[18.12.2012].

CBRC (2007a): *商业银行操作风险管理指引 Guidelines on operational risk management of commercial banks,* available: http://www.cbrc.gov.cn/chinese/home/ docDOC_ ReadView/20070601320CAD62F1FA24FDFF34234E7AC83D00.html[18.6.2012].

CBRC (2007b): *中国银行业监督管理委员会 2006 年报 China Banking Regulatory Commission annual report 2006,* available: http://www.cbrc.gov.cn/chinese/ home/ docView/20070629B5792401322741CBFFF0431894CBC500.html[7.8.2012].

CBRC (2007c): *商业银行信息披露办法 Rules on information disclosure of commercial banks,* available: http://www.cbrc.gov.cn/chinese/home/docDOC_ReadView/20070725 83E55CE5F68A0FE1FF108FFE117FEC00.html[28.6.2012].

CBRC (2007d): *中国银监会关于印发《贷款风险分类指引》的通知 Notice of the CBRC on issuing "Guidelines on risk-based loan classification",* available: http://www. cbrc.gov.cn/upload/zwgk/ml3/2/5-2-9.doc[24.11.2012].

CBRC (2007e): *Rules on monitoring and assessment of non-performing assets of Rural Credit Cooperatives,* available: http://www.cbrc.gov.cn/EngdocView.do?docID=2007 121936894FDEFD7E5F73FF72E29C28602C00[25.11.2012].

CBRC (2007f): *NPLs of commercial banks as of end-2006*, available: http://www.cbrc
.gov.cn/EngdocView.do?docID=20070212B7F451E045DD251AFFB4C2512EB89E00[
18.12.2012].

CBRC (2007g): 中国银监会关于中国邮政储蓄银行开办邮政储蓄定期存单小额质押贷
款业务的批复 *Reply of the CBRC to the application of the PSBC for opening of pledged
loan business with time deposit certificate*, available: http://www.cbrc.gov.cn/ gov-
View_935EC202CA514682B0C98CF6F7D4984A.html[27.8.2013].

CBRC (2007h): *Provisional rules governing lending companies*, available: http://www.
cbrc.gov.cn/EngdocView.do?docID=20070921F39E975515E821F8FF1FF642A511E10
0[3.4.2012].

CBRC (2007i): *Provisional rules governing village and township banks*, available:
http://www.cbrc.gov.cn/govView_5B433BAF88B94712B5E392E3A621052D.html
[3.4.2012].

CBRC (2007j): *Provisional rules governing rural mutual credit cooperatives*, available:
http://www.cbrc.gov.cn/chinese/home/docDOC_ReadView/200701297EC45E   D7B
6693ACCFFBE6C825759A000.html[3.4.2012].

CBRC (2008a): 中国银行业监督管理委员会, 中国人民银行关于小额贷款公司试点的
指导意见 *Guiding opinions of the CBRC and the PBC on the pilot program of microfinance companies*, available: http://www.cbrc.gov.cn/chinese/home/ docDOC_Read
View/2008050844C6FDE83536CF44FFF6E85E5BC32C00.html[6.8.2012].

CBRC (2008b): 中国银行业监督管理委员会 2007 年报 *China Banking Regulatory Commission annual report 2007*, available: http://www.cbrc.gov.cn/chinese/ home/docView/
200804300FB630DC553E65ABFF13F202A6743900.html[20.8.2012].

CBRC (2008c): *NPLs of commercial banks as of end-2007*, available: http://www.
cbrc.gov.cn/EngdocView.do?docID=2007051774830DBD1F20010BFFD7F4A6791F6F
00[18.12.2012].

CBRC (2009a): 商业银行流动性风险管理指引 *Guidelines on liquidity risk management
of commercial banks*, available: http://www.cbrc.gov.cn/EngdocView.do?doc ID=2009
11161A02DF6ACF9A64F1FF37E38D9EFBDA00[21.6.2012].

CBRC (2009b): 中国银行也监督管理委员会 2008 年报 *China Banking Regulatory Commission annual report 2008*, available: http://www.cbrc.gov.cn/chinese/ home/
docView/200906016A540A030280DDDCFF4762FBD0BA4F00.html[7.8.2012].

CBRC (2009c): 中国银监会关于完善商业银行资本补充机制的通知 *Notice of the CBRC
on mechanisms to perfect commercial banks' capital buffer*, available: http://www.
cbrc.gov.cn/govView_7BFF4DC1F6164F33B01E31FEB69E24E9.html[24.11.2012].

CBRC (2009d): *NPLs of commercial banks as of end-2008*, available: http://www.
cbrc.gov.cn/EngdocView.do?docID=20100222323E0A5E521A1F67FF8F7003C2936B0
0[18.12.2012].

CBRC (2010a): 中国银行业监督管理委员会 2009 年报 *China Banking Regulatory Commission annual report 2008*, available: http://www.cbrc.gov.cn/chinese/ home/doc
View/20100615A314C942DEE7DD34FF395FFCEB671E00.html[7.8.2012].

CBRC (2010b): *NPLs of commercial banks as of end-2009*, available: http://www.
cbrc.gov.cn/EngdocView.do?docID=20100222BE211C70FD4E697EFF99B30569CE9A
00[18.12.2012].

CBRC (2010c): *The CBRC issues the Guiding opinions on merger, acquisition and reorganization of high-risk Rural Credit Cooperatives*, available: http://www.cbrc.gov.cn/ EngdocView.do?docID=201009158789E964EC93CAE1FF0EA048DA21BD00 [13.6.2013].

CBRC (2010d): 中国银监会关于加快推进农村信用金融机构股权改造的指导意见 *Guiding opinions of the CBRC on accelerating the shareholding transformation of rural cooperative financial institutions*, available: http://www.cbrc.gov.cn/govView_9EAE6F 24534C4E55BD442F3134563DFF.html[18.6.2013].

CBRC (2011a): 中国银行业实施新监管标准指导意见 *Guiding opinions on the implementation of "New regulatory standards in China's banking industry"*, available: http://www. gov.cn/gzdt/2011-05/03/content_1857048.htm [5.6.2012].

CBRC (2011b): *The CBRC responded to questions of the press relating to the Guiding opinions on the implementation of "New regulatory standards in China's banking industry"*, available: http://www.cbrc.gov.cn/EngdocView.do?docID=20110613FCE47ABD 05FA4204EF5BCBC854991A00[9.6.2012].

CBRC (2011c): *Guidelines on corporate governance of commercial banks (consultative document)*, available: http://www.cbrc.gov.cn/EngdocView.do?docID=20110726E 3B31F1963766665FFCB624208EAB400[2.7.2012].

CBRC (2011d): *The CBRC solicits public opinions on the rules governing liquidity risk of commercial banks (tentative)*, available: http://www.cbrc.gov.cn/ EngdocView.do? docID=20111104C69BB4F212475941FF23F49DB8002E00[4.6.2012].

CBRC (2011e): 中国银行业监督管理委员会 2010 年报 *China Banking Regulatory Commission annual report 2010*, available: http://www.cbrc.gov.cn/chinese/ home/ docView/20110329105207FCE245635EFF756F4AAAAA8900.html[7.8.2012].

CBRC (2012a): 中国银行业监督管理委员会 2011 年报 *China Banking Regulatory Commission annual report 2011*, available: http://www.cbrc.gov.cn/chinese/ home/docView/ 4DE6AD136C6E4F99B9883B7672674FC3.html[7.8.2012].

CBRC (2012b): 商业银行资本管理办法（试行）*Regulation governing capital of commercial banks (tentative)*, available: http://www.cbrc.gov.cn/chinese/home/ docView/ 79B4B184117B47A59CB9C47D0C199341.html[25.9.2012].

CBRC (2012c): 商业银行公司治理指引（征求意见稿）*Guidelines on corporate governance of commercial banks (consultative document)*, available: http://www. cbrc.gov.cn/EngdocView.do?docID=20110726E3B31F1963766665FFCB624208EAB40 0[2.10.2012].

CBRC (2012d): 商业银行贷款损失准备管理办法 *Regulation governing credit loss provision of commercial banks*, available: http://www.cbrc.gov.cn/chinese/home/ doc DOC_ReadView/20111008AA06CE798DC8CB04FF45A8AA68B67200.html[11.12.20 12].

CBRC (2013a): 多层次、较完善的农村金融服务体系已初步形成 *A multi-level and good-performing rural financial service system has taken shape*, available: http://www.cbrc.gov.cn/chinese/home/docView/2C08078B4A5845EBB24DFC07FEEC 1490.html[6.9.2013].

CBRC (2013b): 中国银行业监督管理委员会 2012 年报 *China Banking Regulatory Commission annual report 2012*, available: http://www.cbrc.gov.cn/chinese/home/docView/18492CCBDD04435A8BFAB3FF6F2CA51C.html[11.9.2013].

Chen, L. (2004): "Practical experience with rural commercial banks: a case study of the reform of rural credit co-operatives in China's Jiangsu province", in: OECD (ed.), *Rural Finance and Credit Infrastructure in China*, available: http://www.chinability.com/Rural%20Finance%20and%20Credit%20Infrastructure%20in%20China.pdf[26.7.2011].

Chen, X. (2011):制度变迁中的农户金融合作行为研究 *Study on behavior of farmers' financial cooperation in the institutional change process*, Beijing: People's Publishing House.

Chen, Y. (2009): *Introduction of the Postal Savings Bank of China*, available: http://postfi.files.wordpress.com/2009/11/15-introduction-of-the-postal-savings-bank-of-chinaby-chen-ying.pdf[24.8.2013].

Cheng, Y. (2007): *Building pro-rural economic institutions in China - what can the reforms of Rural Credit Cooperatives achieve?* Available: http://www.networkideas.org/ideasact/jun07/Beijing_Conference_07/Yuk_Shing_Cheng.pdf[13.5.2013].

China Association of Microfinance Team (2010): "Workshop report: a glimpse at the microfinance industry in China". In: World Microfinance Forum Geneva (ed.), *Microfinance in China*, available: http://www.microfinanceforum.org/wp-content/uploads/2012/03/ChinaCompendium-eVersion.pdf[20.8.2013].

China Banking Association (2011): *Research on the development of village and township banks (VTBs) in China*, available: http://www.microfinanceforum.org/ cm_data/111110_VTB_study.pdf[14.4.2012].

China Post Group (2008): *China Post Group annual report 2007*, available: http://www.chinapost.com.cn/36/161/187/index.html[25.8.2013].

China Post Group (2009): *China Post Group annual report 2008*, available: http://www.chinapost.com.cn/36/161/187/index.html[25.8.2013].

China Post Group (2010): *China Post Group annual report 2009*, available: http://www.chinapost.com.cn/36/161/187/index.html[25.8.2013].

China Post Group (2011): *China Post Group annual report 2010*, available: http://www.chinapost.com.cn/36/161/187/index.html[25.8.2013].

China Post Group (2012): *China Post Group annual report 2011*, available: http://www.chinapost.com.cn/36/161/187/index.html[25.8.2013].

China Post Group (2013): *China Post Group annual report 2012*, available: http://www.chinapost.com.cn/report/2012-nb/index.html[25.8.2013].

China Rural Finance Association (2008): *30 years of Chinese rural finance's development and reform*, Beijing: China Financial Publishing House.

Cong, M. / Li, X. (2009): *Reengineering of Rural Credit Cooperatives - report on the reform of Rural Credit Cooperatives*, Beijing: China Legal Publishing House.

Cousin, V. (2011): *Banking in China (2nd edition)*, London: Palgrave Macmillan.

Delatte, A. (unknown): *Monetary Policy and macro-control in China: the actual impact of window guidance*, available: http://www.hkimr.org/cms/upload/seminar _app/sem_paper _0_262_Delatte07.pdf[21.6.2012].

Deloitte China (2013): *2012 China banking industry top ten trends and outlook - enhancing capital management, meeting new challenges*, available: http://www.deloitte.com/view/ en_CN/cn/ind/gfsi/1b0bdd6d8b186310VgnVCM3000001c56f00aRCRD.htm[1.6.2013].

Deng, H. (2009): *Banking supervision and its regulations - comparative study between U.S. and China*, avaialble: http://scholarship.law.cornell.edu/lps_clacp/32/ [20.12.2013].

Deng, Y. (2011): *CBRC's supervision of China's banking industry*, available: http://archive.unctad.org/sections/wcmu/docs/cImem3_3rd_S4_Deng.pdf[26.5.2012].

Deutsche Bundesbank: *Liquidity risk management practices at selected German credit institutions*, available: http://www.bundesbank.de/Redaktion/EN/Downloads/Core_business_ areas/Banking_supervision/PDF/liquidity_risk_management_practices_at_selected_ german_credit_institutions.pdf?__blob=publicationFile[18.9.2012].

Dong, X. (2012): 中国银行风险综合评估与宏观审慎监管 *Comprehensive evaluation and macroeconomic supervision of Chinese banking risks*, available: http://views.ce.cn/view/ ent/201205/18/t20120518_23333625.shtml[21.6.2012].

Du, C. (2001): 邮政储蓄制度安排与改革的考察 *Study on the postal savings system and its reform*, available: http://www.cenet.org.cn/cn/CEAC/%E7%AC% AC%E4%B8% 89%E5%B1%8A%E5%85%A5%E9%80%89%E8%AE%BA%E6%96%87/%E5%88% B6%E5%BA%A6%E7%BB%8F%E6%B5%8E%E5%AD%A6/%E6%9D%9C%E5%B 4%87%E4%B8%9C%E9%82%AE%E6%94%BF%E5%82%A8%E8%93%84%E5%88 %B6%E5%BA%A6%E5%AE%89%E6%8E%92%E4%B8%8E%E6%94%B9%E9%9D %A9%E7%9A%84%E8%80%83%E5%AF%9F.doc[25.8.2013].

Du, X. (2010a): "The current situation and future prospects for microfinance in China", in: World Microfinance Forum Geneva (ed.), *Microfinance in China*, available: http://www.microfinanceforum.org/wp-content/uploads/2012/03/ChinaCompendium-eVersion.pdf[20.8.2013].

Du, X. (2010b): "The current supply of microfinance services in China", in: World Microfinance Forum Geneva (ed.), *Microfinance in China*, available: http://www.micro finance forum.org/wp-content/uploads/2012/03/ChinaCompendium-eVersion.pdf[20.8.2013].

European Central Bank (unknown): *The role of central banks in prudential supervision*, available: http://www.ecb.int/pub/pdf/other/prudentialsupcbrole_en.pdf[21.6.2012].

Fan, Z. / Zhao, Y. / Yang, X. (2012): 我国商业银行公司治理特点与未来走向 *Charisteristics and future trend of corporate governance of Chinese commercial banks*, available: http://finance.sina.com.cn/stock/t/20121016/022013375493.shtml [7.2.2013].

Feder, G. / Lau, L. J. / Justin, J. Y. / Luo, X. (1990): *The relationship between credit and productivity in Chinese agriculture: a microeconomic model of disequilibrium*, available: http://www.jstor.org/stable/10.2307/1242524[1.11.2011].

Forbes (2011): *25 best county-level cities in mainland China in 2011*, available: http://www.forbeschina.com/list/1362[15. 4.2012].

Gale, F. (2009): "Financial reforms push capital to the countryside", *The Chinese Economy*, Vol. 42(5), pp. 58-78.

Gleeson, S. (2010): *International regulation of banking - Basel II: capital and risk require-ments*, New York: Oxford University Press.

Gross, K. (2007): *Equity ownership and performance*, Heidelberg: Physica-Verlag.

Guo, X. / Henehan, B. / Schmit, T. (2007): *Rural supply and marketing cooperatives in China: historical development, problems and reform*, available: http://ncera.aae. wisc.edu/Events/2007meeting/china_paper.pdf[14.3.2013].

Han, J. (2004): "The Creation of a favourable environment for investment in rural China: current situation and future prospects", in: OECD (ed.), *Rural Finance and Credit Infrastructure in China*, available: http://www.chinability com/Rural% 20Finance%20 and%20Credit%20Infrastructure%20in%20China.pdf[26.7.2011].

Han, J. (2008): 中国经济改革三十年 - 农村经济卷 *Thirty years of Chinese economic reform - volume of rural economy*, Chongqing: Chongqing Unversity Press.

Han, J. et al. (2009): *Survey on China's rural finance*, Shanghai: Shanghai Yuandong Publishing House.

He, G. (2005): 农村信用社改革中的股权设置与管理结构 *Shareholding settings and cor-porate governance of RCCs in the reform process*, available: http://www.usc.cuhk. edu.hk/PaperCollection/Details.aspx?id=3736[6.7.2013].

He, G. (2010): "An analysis of microfinance demand in China", in: World Microfinance Fo-rum Geneva (ed.), Microfinance in China, available: http://www.microfinance fo-rum.org/wp-content/uploads/2012/03/ChinaCompendium-eVersion.pdf[20.8.2013].

He, J. (2006): 平遥小额贷款公司紧急输血 三个月放贷800多万 *Microcredit companies in Pingyao conducted urgend blood transfution, in three months they granted credits in amount of over RMB 8 million*, available: http://finance.sina.com. cn/g/20060408 /18082485461.shtml[16.5.2012].

Hope, N. / Hu, F. (2006): *Reforming China's banking system: how much can foreign strate-gic investment help?* Available: http://siepr.stanford.edu/publicationsprofile/1097 [12.12.2011].

Hu, B. et al (2010): 江苏江阴农村商业银行考察 *Field research on the development of Jiangsu Jiangyin Rural Commercial Bank*, Beijing: Economy & Management Publishing House.

Hu, R. (2010): 小额贷款公司资本突破800亿 *Registered capital of microcredit compa-nies exceeded RMB 80 billion*, available: http://finance.sina.com.cn/money/bank/ bank_hydt/20100326/21327642443.shtml[16.5.2012].

International Centre for Financial Regulation ICFR (2010): *Overview of China's regulatory organizational structure and process*, available: http://www.icffr.org/getdoc/ 7e756cdf-e7a6-4c9a-9317bccceb0ede07/Overview-of-China-s-organisation-and-financial reg.aspx[25.5.2012].

IFAD (2001): *Rural financial services*, available: http://www.ifad.org/evaluation/ pub-lic_html/eksyst/doc/thematic/pi/cn/china.pdf[30. 4. 2012].

Jia, X. / Guo, P. (2007): *Evolution of rural financial market in China: an institutional "Lock in" or gradualism?* Available: http://ageconsearch.umn.edu/bitstream/ 7944/1/pp07ji01 .pdf[30. 4.2012].

Jing, N. / Li, S. / Chen, S. (2004): 我国商业银行的资本充足率水平分析 *Analysis of capital adequacy level of Chinese commercial banks*, available: http://www.cnki.com.cn/Article/CJFDTotal-ZJJR200407007.htm[14.9.2012].

KPMG (2012): *Evolving banking regulation - a long journey ahead - the outlook for 2012*, available: http://www.kpmg.com/cn/en/IssuesAndInsights/ ArticlesPublications/Documents/Evolving-Banking-Regulation-Outlook2012-O-201112.pdf[16.5.2012].

Li, M. / Li, X. (2008): 农村信用社贷款竞价问题研究 *Study on the credit pricing of RCCs*, Beijing: China Economic Publishing House.

Li, X. (2009): 中国农村商业银行发展研究 "Study on the RCBs' development in China", *Academic Forum*, General No. 223, pp. 96-100.

Lin, J. Y. (1998): "Agricultural development and reform in China", in: Eicher, C. K. / Staatz, J. M. (eds.), *International agricultural development (3rd Edition)*, Baltimore: The Johns Hopkins University Press.

Liu, M. (2007): *Liu Mingkang's Vision of Rural China's Financial Reform*, available: http://english.caijing.com.cn/2007-05-15/100042921.html [23.8.2011].

Liu, J. / Yang, S. / Zhao, D. et al. (2008): 中国农村金融发展研究 *Study on the development situation of chinese rural finance*, Beijing: Tsinghua University Press.

Liu, L. / Wang, B. (2006): 国有商业银行不良贷款处置迟缓现象分析 *Analysis of slow disposal of NPLs in SOCBs*, available: http://wenku.baidu.com/view/ 067e86778e9951e79b89270b.html [2.11.2012].

Liu, M. / Xu, Z. / Yu, J. / Zhou, S. / Zhao, Y.(2005): "Market-led Reforms of China's Rural Credit Cooperatives: A Proposal", *Journal of Finance Rearch,* 2005 Nr. 5, pp. 99-113.

Liu, W. (2011): *The research on the internal control system of Rural Credit Cooperatives*, Beijing: China Agricultural University Press.

Liu, Y. (2011):我国农村信用社法人治理结构的理论基础：以治理目的与特殊性为视角 *Theoretical foundation of RCCs' corporate governance structure from the perspective of purpose and specificity of RCCs' governance*, available: http://www.nongxinyin.com/pay/html/DFEDA4BD77654D53973786786E2205ED.htm[8.7.2013].

Ma, X. (2004): "The difficulties and policy reform in China's rural finance", in: OECD (ed.), *Rural finance and credit infrastructure in China*, available: http://www.chinability.com/Rural%20Finance%20and%20Credit%20Infrastructure%20in%20China.pdf[26.7.2011].

Marks, C. (2010): "Rural banking in China", in: *Asia focus*, available: http://www.frbsf.org/ publications/banking/asiafocus/2010/may.pdf[30.4.2012].

Meyer, R. / Nagarajan, G. (2000): *Rural financial markets in Asia: policies, paradigms, and performance*, New York: Oxford University Press.

Ministry of Finance (1993): 财政部关于印发《金融保险企业财务制度》的通知 *Notice of the Ministry of Finance on issuing "Accounting rules of financial and insurance companies"*, available: http://www.ndcnc.gov.cn/datalib/2003/PolicyLaw/ DL/DL-12322 [7.12.2012].

Mishkin, F. S. (2001): *Prudential Supervision: why is it important and what are the issues?* Available: http://www.nber.org/chapters/c10756.pdf[21.6.2012].

Mu, Z. (2011):*农村信用社法人治理与管理体制研究 Study on the legal person right and management system reform of RCCs*, Beijing: China Financial Publishing House.

National Bureau of Statistics of China (unknown): *Chinese statistical year book*, available: http://www.stats.gov.cn/tjsj/[30. 4. 2012].

OECD (2004): *Rural finance and credit infrastructure in China*, available: http://www.chinability.com/Rural%20Finance%20and%20Credit%20Infrastructure%20in%20China.pdf [30. 4. 2012].

Ong, L. (2006): "Multiple principals and collective action: China's Rural Credit Cooperatives and poor households' access to credit", *Journal of East Asian Studies*, 2006 Nr.6, pp. 177-204.

ORACLE Financial Services (2009): *Liquidity risk management in financial services: strategies for success*, available: http://www.oracle.com/us/industries/financial-services/045994.pdf [18.9.2012].

Packer, F. / Zhu, H. (2012): *Loan loss provisioning practices in Asian banks*, BIS working papers, available: http://www.bis.org/publ/work375.pdf[17.9.2012].

PBC (unknown a): *Institutional arrangement of the PBC*, available: http://www.pbc. gov.cn/publish/english/968/index.html[8.9.2013].

PBC (unknown b): *Management and organizational structure of the PBC*, available: http://www.pbc.gov.cn/publish/english/969/index.html[8.9.2013].

PBC (1995a): *Law on the People's Bank of China*, available: http://www.pbc.gov.cn/rhwg/19981801.htm[14.6.2012].

PBC (1995b): *中华人民共和国商业银行法 Law of the People's Republic of China on commercial banks*, available: http://www.pbc.gov.cn/publish/tiaofasi/272/ 1384/13841 /13841.html [14.6.2012].

PBC (1996): *General rules for loans*, available: http://money.163.com/08/0623/15/4F4Q1EI300251OB6.html[8.10.2012].

PBC (1997a): *农村信用合作社管理规定 Administrative provisions on RCCs*, available: http://www.pbc.gov.cn/rhwg/971201f1.htm[1.6.2012].

PBC (1997b): *关于印发《农村信用合作社管理规定》和《农村信用合作县级联合社管理规定》的通知 Notice of the PBC on the issuance of "Provisions concerning management of RCCs" and "Provisions concerning management of county RCC unions"*, available: http://www.law-lib.com/law/law_view.asp?id=13472[17.7.2013].

PBC (2001): *贷款风险分类指导原则 Guidelines on risk-based loan classification*, available: http://www.china.com.cn/chinese/PI-c/92034.htm [25.11.2012].

PBC (2002): *Guidance on provisioning for loan losses*, available: http://www. for68.com/new/2007/1/li4057143620192170026290-0.htm[27.12.2012].

PBC (2003a): *中华人民共和国人民银行法（修正）Law on the People's Bank of China (revised)*, available: http://www.pbc.gov.cn/publish/zhengwugongkai/501/ 1811/18117/18117_.html[24.6.2012].

PBC (2003b): *中国人民银行关于印发《农村信用社改革试点专项中央银行票据操作办法》和《农村信用社改革试点专项借款管理办法》的通知 Notice of the PBC on the issuance of "Operational rules of PBC's special notes for RCCs in the pilot reform" and*

"Management rules of special lending for RCC in the pilot reform", available: http://china.findlaw.cn/fagui/p_1/179022.html[12.5.2013].

PBC (2004): 中国人民银行关于印发《农村信用社改革试点资金支持方案实施与考核指引》的通知 *Notice of the PBC on issuance of "Guidelines of implementation and evaluation of financial support program in RCC pilot reform regions"*, available: http://baike.baidu.com/view/2683596.htm[14.5.2013].

PBC (2011): 中国农村金融服务报告 2010 *China rural finance service report 2010*, Beijing: China Financial Publishing House.

PBC (2012a): 2011 年小额贷款公司数据统计报告 *Statistic report of microfinance companies in 2011*, available: http://www.pbc.gov.cn/publish/goutongjiaoliu/524/2012/20120220150038305800973/20120220150038305800973_.html[18.8.2013].

PBC (2012b): 2012 年上半年小额贷款公司数据统计报告 *Statistic report of microfinance companies in the first half of 2012*, available: http://www.pbc.gov.cn/publish/ diaochatongjisi/3172/2012/20120730155358762590662/20120730155358762590662_.html[6.8. 2012].

PBC (2013a): 2012 年小额贷款公司数据统计报告 *Statistic report of microfinance companies in 2012*, available: http://www.pbc.gov.cn/publish/diaochatongjisi/ 3172/2013/20130201184822380850461/20130201184822380850461_.html[18.8.2013].

PBC (2013b): 2013 年上半年小额贷款公司数据统计报告 *Statistic report of microfinance companies in the first half of 2013*, available: http://www.pbc.gov.cn/ pulish/ goutongjiaoliu/524/2013/20130729150845454245503/20130729150845454245503 _.html [18.8.2013].

PBC (2013c): 2012 年中国区域金融运行报告 *China regional financial performance report 2012*, available: http://www.pbc.gov.cn/image_public/UserFiles/goutongjiao liu/upload/File/2012/%E5%B9%B4%E4%B8%AD%E5%9B%BD%E5%8C%BA%E5% 9F%9F%E9%87%91%E8%9E%8D%E8%BF%90%E8%A1%8C%E6%8A%A5%E5%9 1%8A%E4%B8%BB%E6%8A%A5%E5%91%8A.pdf[18.8.2013].

PBC (2013d): 中国农村金融服务报告 2012（摘要）*China rural finance service report 2012 (abstract)*, available: http://www.pbc.gov.cn/publish/goutongjiaoliu/524/ 2013/2013 0403154858727632654/20130403154858727632654_.html[20.8.2013].

PBC / CBRC (2007): 关于建立《涉农贷款专项统计制度》的通知 *Notice of the PBC and the CBRC on the establishment of "The specific statistical system of agriculture-related loans"*, available: http://www.shui5.cn/article/b9/45737.html[21.8. 2013].

PBC / CBRC (2008): *Opinions of the PBC and the CBRC on accelerating the innovation of financial products and services in rural areas*, available: http://www.gov.cn/ gong-bao/content/2009/content_1266000.htm[1.9.2013].

PSBC (2013a): *Agro-related financial service report 2012*, available: http://www.psbc. com/portal/zh_CN/upload/File/youchuxinwen/2012sannongjinrongfuwubaogao.pdf[21.8 .2013].

PSBC (2013b): *Brief introduction of the PSBC*, available: http://www.psbc.com/portal /zh_CN/PsbcDemeanour/PsbcDemeanour/37061.html[24.8.2013].

Reaz, M. M. (2009): "Improving corporate governance of banks: issues and experience from Bangladesh", in: Arun / Turner (ed.), *Corporate governance and development - re-*

form, financial systems and legal frameworks, Cheltenham & Northampton: Edward El-gar Publishing Limited.

Rochet, J. (2008): *Why are there so many banking crises? - the politics and policy of bank regulation*, Princeton: Prinston Unversity Press.

Rymanowska, P. (2006): *The Basel I and Basel II accords: the comparison of the models and economical conclusions*, available: http://www.math.vu.nl/~sbhulai/ theses/thesis-rymanowska.pdf[17.9.2012].

Scott, D. / Druschel, K. (2004): "Institutional issures and prerequisites for efficient savings mobilization and allocation in rural and less developed regions in China", in: OECD (ed.), *Rural finance and credit infrastructure in China*, available: http://www .chinability.com/Rural%20Finance%20and%20Credit%20Infrastructure%20in%20China .pdf[26.7.2011].

Shen, M. / Huang, J. et al. (2010): "Financial reform and transition in China: a study of the evolution of banks in rural China", *Agricultural Finance Review*, Vol. 70(3), pp. 305-332.

Shenzhen Microfinance Industry Association (2013): *2012 年年度全国小额贷款行业概况统计分析 Statistical Analysis of microfinance industry in China 2012*, available: http://www.szmfa.org.cn/_d276116760.htm[5.9.2013].

Shi, H. (2005): *国有商业银行账面不良贷款、调整因素和严重程度：1994 - 2004 NPLs of SOCBs on the balance sheet, their adjustment factors and the severeness of NPLs from 1994 to 2004*, available: http://ishare.iask.sina.com.cn/f/23529843.html [30.11.2012].

Soh K. / Thomas D. (2010): *Chongqing Rural raises $1.35 billion in HK IPO: sources*, available: http://www.reuters.com/article/2010/12/09/us-chongqing-pricing-idUST RE6B81F720101209[16.9.2013].

Söhlke, T. (2002): *Regulatorische Erfassung des Kreditrisikos*, Wiesbaden: Gabler Publishing House.

Song, L. / Wang, J. (2007): 山东省农村信用社产权改革绩效评价的实证研究 "An empirical study of property rights' reform of Rural Credit Cooperatives in Shandong Province", *Issues in Agricultural Economy*, Vol. 2007(8), pp70-75.

Subrahmanyam, V. (2011): *City and rural commercial banks in China: the new battlefield in Chinese banking?* Available: http://www.chinacenter.net/city-and-rural-commercial-banks-in-china-the-new-battlefield-in-chinese-banking/[5.8.2013].

Sun, T. (2010): "The policy and legal framework for microfinance in China", in: World Microfinance Forum Geneva (ed.), *Microfinance in China*, available: http://www.microfinanceforum.org/wp-content/uploads/2012/03/ChinaCompendium-eVersion.pdf[20.8.2013].

State Council of the PRC (1993): *国务院关于金融体制改革的决定 Decision of the State Council on reform of the financial system*, available: http://news.xinhuanet .com/ziliao/2005-03/17/content_2709610.htm [19.8.2013].

State Council of the PRC (1996): *国务院关于农村金融体制改革的决定 Decision of the State Council on Chinese rural financial reform*, available: http://www.pbc.gov .cn/rhwg/961401.htm[15.1.2013].

State Council of the PRC (2003): 关于深化农村信用社改革试点方案的通知 *Scheme for deepening the pilot reform of Rural Credit Cooperatives*, available: http://www.gov.cn/zwgk/2005-08/13/content_22249.htm[14.2.2011].

State Council of the PRC (2004): 关于进一步深化农村信用社改革试点的意见 *Opinions on further deepening the pilot reform of Rural Credit Cooperatives*, available: http://www.gov.cn/gongbao/content/2004/content_62965.htm[14.2.2011].

Statistics Bureau of Jiangsu Province (2012): 从数字看2011年的江苏 *A statistical overview of Jiangsu Province in 2011*, available: http://www.jssb.gov.cn/ jssq/jjgk/ 201112/t20111208_21846.htm [10.3.2013].

Stiglitz, J. E. (1994): *The role of the State in financial markets (proceedings of the World Bank Annual Conference on Development Economics, 1993)*, Washington, D.C.: The World Bank.

Tanaka, M. (2002): *How do bank capital and capital adequacy regulation affect the monetary transmission mechanism?* Avaialble: http://www.cesifo-group.de/portal/ pls/portal/ifo_applications.switches.DocLinkIfoDL?getDoc=cesifo_wp799.pdf.[29.11.20 12].

Tarullo, D. K. (2008): *Banking on Basel - the future of international financial regualtion*, Washington: Peterson Institute for International Economics.

Thompson, G. J. (1996): *Prudential supervision and the changing financial system*, available: http://www.rba.gov.au/publications/bulletin/1996/apr/pdf/bu-0496-3.pdf [21. 6.2012].

Tirole, J. (2006): *The theory of corporate finance*, Princeton: Princeton University Press.

Van Empel, G. / Smit, L. (2004): "Development of sustainable credit co-operatives in China", in: OECD (ed.), *Rural finance and credit infrastructure in China*, available: http://www.chinability.com/Rural%20Finance%20and%20Credit% 20Infrastructure%20in%20China.pdf[26.7.2011].

Vento, G. A. (2009): *Bank liquidity risk management and supervision: which lessons from recent market turmoil?* Available: http://www.eurojournals.com/ jmib_10_06.pdf [18.9.2012].

Von Pischke, J. D. / Adams, D. W. / Donald, G. (1983): *Rural financial markets in developing countries: their use and abuse*, Baltimore MD: Johns Hopkins University Press.

Wan, J. (unknown): 我国农村信用社改革模式的探讨 *Discussion about the reform model of RCCs in China*, available: http://www.whdachengnet.com/wenku/ShowAr ticle.asp?ArticleID=246[8.4.2013].

Wang, W. (2004): "The regulatory framework for Rural Credit Cooperatives: the role of Chinese supervisory authorities", *in:* OECD (ed.) *Rural Finance and Credit Infrastructure in China*, available: http://www.chinability.com/Rural%20Finance %20 and%20Credit%20Infrastructure%20in%20China.pdf[26.7.2011].

Wang, X. (2009): *On the rural finance reform of China*, Beijing: China Financial Publishing House.

Wang, S. (2009): 信用重建 *Reconstruction of creditability in rural areas*, Beijing: China Development Press.

Wang, P. (2012): 农村金融破与立 "Rural finance's destroy and reestablishment in China", *Caijing Magzine*, supplement 2012(4).

Wang, S. / Gao, G. (2009): *Study of rural credit cooperatives in Tianjin*, Beijing: Economy & Management Publishing House.

Wang, H. / Hu, G. (2004): 股权结构在公司治理中的作用及效率—文献回顾及基于中国上市公司的未来研究方向 *The role and efficiency of shareholding structure in corporate governance - a literature review and further research directions based on Chinese listed companies*, available: http://202.112.126.101/jpkc/shang xueyuanzhou/jpkc_ cwglx/jxnr/xrwj_3.pdf[27.1.2013].

Wang, S. / Qiao, Y. et al. (2008): *Rural finance*, Beijing: Peking University Press.

Weston, R. (1980): *Domestic and multinational banking - the effects of monetary policy*, London: Croom Helm Ltd.

Wu, H. X. (1997): *Reform in China's agriculture – trade implications*, available: http://www.dfat.gov.au/publications/catalogue/eaaubp9.pdf[12.12.2011].

Wu, X. (2010): 中国银行业资本充足率高时因资本市场发展差 *The reason of high CAR level in Chinese banking industry lies in the poor development of Chinese capital market*, available: http://finance.ifeng.com/bank/special/2010zgyhj/20100917/ 2632920.shtml [9.11.2012].

Xi, J. / Ru, S. (2011): 陕西省农村信用社改革绩效评价 — 基于陕西省 8 个县农村信用社的实地调查 "Research on the achievements of RCCs reforms of Shaanxi Province - based on the field investigation of RCCs in eight counties of Shaanxi", *Journal of Northwest A & F University (Social Science Edition)*, Vol. 11(2), pp. 37-43.

Xi, S. / Zhu, F. / Wang, P. (2012): 农村信用社改革发展的回顾与展望 - 以山东省为例 "Retrospect and Prospect of the reform and development of Rural Credit Cooperatives in Shandong Province", *Shandong Social Sciences*, Nr. 197, pp. 127-130.

Xia, S. (2007): *China's rural credit cooperatives, cooperative or commercial*, available: http://www1.doshisha.ac.jp/~sshinoha/report/2007/2007_china/Papers%20of% 20Renmin%20Unv/Shiyun_Xia%20_2007.pdf [5.10. 2011].

Xiao, Z. (ed.) (2006): 中国金融市场分析与预测 - 2006 年金融金皮书 *Analysis and forecast of the Chinese financial markets - 2006 Finance Gold Book*, Beijing: Economic Sciences Publishing House.

Xie, P. (2003): *Reforms of China's rural credit cooperatives and policy options*, available: http://202.114.32.103/ctdb/UserFile/Inspect/201109020119389.pdf [15.4.2012].

Xie, P. / Xu, Z. / Cheng, E. / Shen M. (2005): *Establishing a framework for sustainable rural finance - demand and supply analysis in Guizhou Province of the People's Republic of China*, available: http://www.microfinancegateway.org/gm/document-1.9.26288 /28110_file_28110.pdf [15.04.2012].

Xie, P. / Xu, Z. / Shen, M. (2006): 农村信用社改革绩效评价 "Performance evaluation of RCC reform", *Journal of Financial Research,* General Nr. 307, pp.23-39.

Xie, Z. (2011): 农村金融理论与实践 *Theory and praxis of rural finance*, Beijing: Peking University Press.

Xinhua News Agency (2009): *China to legalize private in bid to ease rural credit pressure*, available: http://news.xinhuanet.com/english/2009-03/04/content_109437 30.htm [3.8.2011].

Yang, X. (2006): 农村信用社统一法人换汤更要换药 "Unification of legal person of RCCs: a change not only in form but also in essence", *China Co-operation Times*, Nr.2052, pp.3.

Yaron, J. (1994): "What makes rural financial institutions successful?", *The World Bank Research Observer*, Vol. 9 (1), pp.49-70.

Yaron, J. / Benjamin, M. (1997): "Developing rural financial markets", *Journal Finance & Development*, Vol. 34(4), pp.40-43.

Zhang, D. (unknown): 中国国有商业银行改革：一个公司治理结构角度的分析 *Reform of SOCBs in China: Analysis from the perspective of corporate governance*, available: http://www.cenet.org.cn/article.asp?articleid=6368[1.2.2013].

Zhang, H. (2004): "The system of chinese rural financial organisations: achievements, shortcomings an institutional renewal", in: OECD (ed.), *Rural Finance and Credit Infrastructure in China*, available: http://www.chinability.com/Rural%20Finance%20and%20Credit%20Infrastructure%20in%20China.pdf[26.7.2011].

Zhang, T. (2011): 关于国有商业银行不良资产问题研究 *Research on non-performing assets of SOCBs in China*, available: http://www.studa.net/bank/111017/10101026.html[18.12.2012].

Zhang, X. / Zhong, X. / Shen, M. / Cheng, E. (2010): *Rural finance in poverty-stricken areas in the People's Republic of China: balancing government and market*, Mandaluyong City: Asian Development Bank.

Zhang, Y. / Feng, Z. (2005): 对商业银行流动性风险管理的思考 "Reflections on the liquidity management of commercial banks in China", *Exploration and Free Views*, 2005 Nr. 5, pp.32-34.

Zhao, W. (2008): 农村信用社：风险监测与预警研究 *Study on running risk surveillance and early warning system of RCCs*, Beijing: Economic Science Press.

Zhao, Y. (2011): *China's Rural Financial System: Households' Demand for Credit and Recent Reforms*, Oxon: Routledge Publishing House.

Zhou, L. (2009a): 农村资金供求形势的变迁-三十年农村金融改革回顾 "Change of rural capital demand and supply in China - a review of thirty years rural financial reform", *The Chinese Banker*, 2009 Nr.3, pp.33.

Zhou, S. (2009b): 我国农村合作金融机构的区域发展分析与启示 "Analysis of regional development of Chinese rural cooperative financial institutions", *South China Finance*, 2009 Nr.5, pp.34.

Zhou, Y. / Kang, H. (2011): 我国商业银行资本充足率存在的问题及解决办法 "Existing problems of Chinese commercial banks' CAR and their solutions", *Charming China*, 2011 Nr.6, pp.156.

Zhu, X. (2011): *The reform and development of rural finance in China*, available: http://www.adbi.org/files/2011.07.12.cpp.sess2.1.1.xiujie.eng.reform.dev.rural.finance.prc.pdf[14. 10. 2011].

Zuo, X. (unknown): *The development of credit unions in China: past experiences and lessons for the future*, available: http://www.hks.harvard.edu/m-rcbg/Conferences/ financial_sector/PastFailuresoftheCreditUnion.pdf[15.3.2012].

Annex 1: Risk assessment system for JSCBs

The main risks that encounter the banking sector include capital risk, credit risk, profitability risk, liquidity risk, management or operational risk, market risk and so on. A rating system is designed to show the riskiness of a financial institution. The most famous and mature risk rating system is called CAMELS rating system used in the US, in this system, six critical elements of a financial institution's operation, namely capital (C), asset quality (A), management (M), earnings (E), liability management (L) and sensitivity to market (S) are measured (Zhao 2008: 40). The evaluation of the six criteria is based on the results and data gathered through on-site examination and off-site surveillance. When the rating system was first used in the US in 1979, it had only 5 criteria and was called "CAMEL" rating system (Zhao 2008: 40). In 1997, the item "sensitivity to market" was added to the whole system and the system was renamed as "CAMELS" rating system (Zhao 2008: 40). In the Great Britten, the risk rating system "CAMELB" is being applied, in Singapore the risk rating system CAMELOT (Zhao 2008: 60). A rating system is a good method to check the stability of financial institutions and warn them of the possible risks.

Taking the rating system in the US, Singapore, Britain, Hong Kong and other countries and regions as references, China began with the design work of its own banking supervisory rating system in 2001, which also takes the specific situation of China's banking sector into consideration. In February 2004 the "Provisional risk assessment system for JSCBs" was promulgated by the CBRC. This rating system is called "CAMELS+" in the annual report of the CBRC 2006. The criteria that the rating system relays on are similar with the "CAMELS" rating system in the US with the capital adequacy, asset safety, management, earnings, liquidity and sensibility to market as main checking points. Each risk item of these will be scored based on quantitative and qualitative assessment. The scores of each item will then be multiplied with its weight (from 10% to 25%) and added together to build up the final rating score of the JSCB.

Table A1-1: **The quantitative and qualitative indicators used to measure the six rating criteria and the requirements to get full mark**

Rating criteria		Points	Indicator & comments	Points
Capital adequacy	Quant.	60	CAR (>10%)	30
			Tier 1 CAR (>6%)	30
	Qual.	40	Components and quality of bank capital: stability, fully paid in or not	6
			Overall financial status of the bank and its impact on capital: profitability, competitive position, adverse factors	8
			Asset quality and its influence on capital (comparing trends in NPLs/provisions)	8
			Ability of banks to raise capital in markets or from other channels	8
			Management of capital: plans, strategy, forecasting, profit distribution	10

Rating criteria		Points	(Continuation) Indicator & comments	Points
Management Administration	Bank management	50	Fundamental structure of the bank's management: structure, institutions in place and responsibilities	10
			Decision making system of banking corporate governance: qualification of shareholders and directors	10
			Execution system of the bank's corporate governance	10
			Supervision system of the bank's corporate governance	10
	Internal controls	50	Internal control environment and culture (mechanisms, structures, culture)	10
			Risk identification and assessment: risk management procedure and systems	10
			Controlling behavior and responsibilities (business policies, responsibilities, control mechanisms, emergency systems)	10
			Information communications: information sharing, integrity of information	10
			Supervision and correction	10

Rating criteria		Points	(Continuation) Indicator & comments	Points
Liquidity	Quant.	60	Liquidity ratio (>35%)	20
			RMB excessive reserve ratio (>5%): RMB excessive reserves mean RMB reserves after deduction of required reserves	10
			Foreign currency excessive reserve ratio (>5%)	5
			Loan to deposit ratio (<65%): combination of RMB and Foreign Currency	10
			Loan to deposit ratio (<70%): Foreign Currency	5
	Qual.	40	Net interbank borrowing ratio = interbank borrowing ratio − interbank lending ratio (< - 4%)	10
			Composites, development tendency and stability of the bank's capital sources	5
			Assets and liabilities management policy and the capital distribution situation	5
			Management over liquidity	20
			Ability of the bank to meet its liquidity demands through methods of voluntary liabilities	5
			Ability of the bank's managers to effectively identify, monitor and regulate the position status of the bank	5

Source: CBRC 2004b/ Cousin 2011: 236-238

The Table A1-1 gives us a brief introduction of the main items, their indicators and their scores. The whole risk assessment system combines quantitative and qualitative analysis in the way that each dimension of CAMELS+ rating includes both quantitative and qualitative factors, except for management quality. The qualitative analysis is made after collection of complete related information, so that the qualitative assessment is scientific and objective. Each item has the total score of 100 points. The quantitative and the qualitative parts make up a certain percentage in the whole score system. To get a final result, each item should be multiplied with its weight according to its contribution to the evaluation of the final result. The Table A1-2 otherwise shows the weight of each item for the final result and the grading rules with all together 5 levels. We can see that, the item with the highest weight percentage is management situation with 25%. Capital adequacy situation, asset safety situation and earnings situation rank at the second places with 20%. Liquidity situation makes up of 15%. Sensitivity to market was although measured, but not included in the final score. After getting the scores, the assessed financial institutions will be grouped into 5 levels. Financial institutions of level 1 should have a least score of 85 points. Financial institutions in this group are "excellent" ones. Financial institutions with scores between 75 and 85 belong to the second level, which is called "good". Financial institutions with less than 50 points are seen as bad banks.

Table A1-2:   Bank assessment system CAMELS (References for laws 29 in 2005)

Weights	Capital adequacy situation 20% Asset safety situation 20% Management situation 25% Earnings situation 20% Liquidity 15% Sensitivity to market 0% No overriding factor
Overall and single factor assessment	Level 1 Excellent: >85 Level 2 Good: 75 - 85 Level 3 Special Mention: 60 - 75 Level 4 Substandard: 50 - 60 Level 5 Bad: < 50
Period of the assessment	One year
Disclosure	Assessment results will be announced to related sectors and after inspections

Source: Cousin 2011: 32; CBRC 2004b

The results of the banking assessment will be announced to related sectors by the regulatory authorities and won't be published temporarily (CBRC 2004b). Any problem found out during the assessment process should be reported to the bank; the board of directors should urge and supervise the senior management to modify them. The regulatory institutions also use the results to design their supervision work and distribute sources (CBRC 2004b). "For banks whose single operation assessment result is below 3, regulators should strengthen their supervisions and make specific on-the-spot inspections according to circumstances. For banks whose single operation assessment result is below level 4, regulators should inquire its senior management and ask them to lower the bank's risk level. For banks whose single operation assessment result is below 5, regulators should urge them to make plan to improve the bank's risk situation, and execute the plan under the supervision of regulatory institutions" (CBRC 2004b). Data of the current ranking of riskiness of Chinese JSCBs are not available on the CBRC official website.

Annex 2: Core indicators for prudential supervision

On the base of the risk assessment system, core indicators with predictive power to monitor the performance and riskiness of financial institutions were elected and expressed in the document "Core indicators for risk-based supervision of commercial banks (tentative)" of the CBRC in 2005. The main indicators are categorized into three groups according to their functions like risk level indicators, risk migration indicators and risk prevention indicators. To measure the risk level of a financial institution liquidity risk, credit risk, market risk and operational risk are taken into consideration. Risk migration on the other hand is measured through migration rate of loans between performing and all other categories of the loan classification. Risk prevention or risk offsetting is measured by the ability of the bank to make profits to cover losses (Cousin 2011: 33). This is the first time that the Chinese supervisory authority officially gave standards for some main indicators to control risks of financial institutions. The maximum or minimum requirements for these indicators are described in the following table. The Core Indicators took effect in January 2006.

Table A2-1: Core supervisory indicators and standards regulated in "Core indicators for risk-based supervision of commercial banks (tentative)"

Classes of indicators		First level indicators	Second level indicators	Indicator standard
Risk level indicators	Liquidity risk	1.Liquidity ratio		≥25%
		2.Core liability ratio		≥60%
		3.liquidity gap ratio		≥ -10%
	Credit risk	4. Ratio of non-performing assets		≤ 4%
			4.1 NPL ratio	≤ 5%
		5. Credit concentration ratio of a single group client	5.1 Loan concentration ratio of a single client	≤15% ≤10%
		6.Generalized correlation ratio		≤50%
	Market risk	7. Ratio of accumulative open foreign exchange positions		≤20%
		8.Interest rate risk sensibility		
	Operational risk	9. Loss ratio of operational risk		

Classes of indicators		(Continuation) First level indicators	Second level indicators	Indicator standard
Risk migration indicators	Pass loans	10. Migration ratio of pass loans	10.1 Migration ratio of pass loans 10.2 migration ratio of special mention loans	
	NPLs	11. Migration ratio of NPLs	11.1 Migration ratio of sub-standard loans 11.3 Migration ratio of doubt-ful loans	
Risk provision/Offsetting indicators	Profitability	12. Cost/income ratio (C/I ratio)		≤35%
		13.Return on as-sets		≥0.6%
		14.Return on eq-uity		≥11%
	Provision ade-quacy degree	15. Asset loss provision cover-age ratio	15.1 Loan loss provision cov-erage ratio	>100% >100%
	Capital ade-quacy degree	16.CAR	16.1 Core CAR	≥8% ≥4%

Source: CBRC 2005d

These core indicators should also be complied with by RcoBs, urban cred-it cooperatives, RCCs, wholly foreign-funded banks as well as Chinese-foreign joint equity banks, when no separate and special regulations are published for them (CBRC 2005d). An enforcement of the implementation and punishment of institutions which can't fulfill the standards do not ex-ist (CBRC 2005d).